Praise for

UNWRITTEN

"Wow! What can you say about *Unwritten*? John and Lorraine have truly opened their hearts to the world with this book. It's truly a testimony of the grace of God in the midst of tragedy. Every chapter unfolded more of how the Lord sustains, leads, and guides. Through my twenty-year journey of walking with John and Lorraine, I had heard snippets here and there of their story, but I never fully realized the extent of what the Lord had done in the midst of tragedy. I had always admired and looked up to them, but after reading *Unwritten* I value our relationship even more. I would highly recommend this heartwarming story to anyone, and to be blessed by the principles of God's love like you've never been blessed before."

Dr. Evon G. Horton
Senior Pastor
Brownsville Assembly, Pensacola, FL

"For those of us who are always wondering what's next and are continually on the run, this book is a wonderful interruption to consider reality. John and Lorraine have given us a great gift in *Unwritten*. While it contains tools to deal with stress, disappointment, leadership, and our walk with God, it is also a great story. It is a wise and God-filled look back on thirty years of life—life that was interrupted by the most horrific of accidents—and John and Lorraine's honesty in telling the story is breathtaking. Their story holds a severe mercy as they help us understand what it is to sink into the silence of God, and yet find God still writes each day of our future. From their loss we learn that whatever our distress, God is still at work to bring us His very best gifts for our lives."

Lorna Dueck
Executive Producer, *Listen Up TV*
Faith Commentator, *The Globe and Mail*

"I met John and Lorraine when I first began ministry at Skyline. There is something about them that indicates a deeper walk; from their lives surfaces a passion to make a difference with their lives! It is in reading *Unwritten* that the pieces of the puzzle fall into place, and I understand more of what is behind the scenes for them. This is a remarkable story of restored hope for a greater dream, and they draw the reader into the journey as they speak with great transparency and authenticity. Step in, let the surf rise, and ride the wave with them. You will be changed forever!"

Jim Garlow

Senior Pastor, Skyline Wesleyan Church, San Diego, CA

Chairman, Renewing American Leadership (ReAL)

"While working with John and Lorraine for nine years, I experienced their great faith in God and their passion for serving churches across Canada, no matter the challenges ahead of them. Churches there are better off for having been touched by their ministry. This book recounts a significant part of their lives and tells the remarkable story about the faithfulness of God and what God can do with lives that are truly His. I was challenged and deeply encouraged in every dimension of life through reading *Unwritten*."

Gary Schwammlein

Executive Vice President, International Ministries

Willow Creek Association

"John and Lorraine have been a great team for five decades. They have teamed up again to give their insider's story of driving ambition, tragedy, faith, resiliency, enduring love, and a forever trust in God. There is still much unwritten as they prepare for their future. As their son Byron so aptly put it, 'They have courage; they are not quitting; they are not finished yet!'"

R. W. (Bob) Taylor

Management Consulting Professional

Former Assistant Deputy Minister, Alberta Department of Energy

"I started with chapter one and was instantly captivated! This is anointed writing! You both have a God-given ability to take the reader on the roller-coaster ride with you. We felt like we were right there with you, every step of the way! This is the first book I've read that, on the one hand, pulls you into this horrendous experience, but on the other hand enables you to be constantly aware that God is in control, and there is HOPE! Your writing truly brings glory to our Father in heaven! It is our honour to be able to call ourselves friends of such spiritual giants."

Gerry Couchman

Executive Director

Willow Creek Association, South Africa

"From a personal point of view, this must be the most horrific yet hopeful story I have ever read. The Baergens have done an awesome job of blending their stories together and telling them separately but together. I've never been on such a rollercoaster ride of emotions as when I read this book. I was filled with sorrow, awe, anger, and disbelief, yet I felt their strong love of the Lord and their love for one another and their family. I never once felt hopeless, but was continually filled with a sense of awe for the Baergens' mature faith and incredible, God-given strength.

"I believe that every person on planet earth should read this story, as it brings hope, inspiration, a challenge, and a strong reality check. We are always moaning about something, and the Baergens' story truly reminds us that there is always someone else worse off. Their story will certainly bless, encourage, inspire, challenge, motivate, and capture everyone—but above all, it will point them to the One and Only God who brought them through this poignant journey."

Janine Couchman

Event Manager

Willow Creek Association, South Africa

"My friends, John and Lorraine, are two of the most joy-filled and faith-filled people you will meet, and their adventure with God has had everything to do with it! Like many, they lived the good life, but God was preparing them for more. We are invited along as they take us from the death of a dream to the discovery of an even greater one. You will be blessed reading this moving story of tragedy turning to triumph through faith in Jesus Christ."

Dr. Henry Schorr
Senior Pastor
Centre Street Church, Calgary, AB

"'Put a good face on.' 'Be strong.' 'Don't drop your guard.' 'Play your cards close to your chest.' 'People won't follow you if they see your weakness.' John and Loraine, two of Canada's most respected leaders and pastors to pastors, throw aside these common notions and welcome us into the inner corridors of their hearts and lives. As they share their story and personal journey through deep pain, they are real, raw, and gut-wrenchingly honest. In their vulnerability, we see clearly how God can work through tragedy to transform the human heart. *Unwritten* will help all who must face life-altering events that leave them broken and in despair to discover how God can birth new hope and higher dreams for the days yet to be lived."

Tim Day
Senior Pastor
The Meeting House, Oakville, ON

"This book, by my friends John and Lorraine, is full of hope for all who wrestle with the hurts, disappointments, and broken dreams of the past. I was deeply impacted by their story—but more than that, by the God who wants to write a brand new future for us. I will recommend *Unwritten* to all my friends!"

Dan Cochrane
Senior Pastor
Crossroads Church, AB

"This is a riveting, sad, real-life story of setbacks turned into steps forward. It emphatically illustrates the exciting Biblical principle of how God is waiting, wanting, and willing to turn our greatest difficulties into our greatest discoveries—when there is a humble attitude and a persevering faith. Thousands have been positively impacted because of the steadfastness of John and Lorraine in the midst of overwhelming challenges. This book will give hope to the devastated."

L. D. Buckingham
Lead Pastor
Moncton Wesleyan Church, Moncton, NB

"Never assume what the next chapter of your life will be. Be prepared for new realities. This is the gripping story of two leaders who never lost faith, even through tragedy. John and Lorraine remind us that we are writing today the life foundations which will shape our unwritten tomorrows. A powerful read that touched me profoundly."

Mark Goring
Chaplain
Catholic Chaplaincy at York University

"Even if I didn't know John and Lorraine, I would be mesmerized by their story. Knowing them, I am blown away by their capacity to mine their own experience for *so many* transferable insights. They are a winsome couple whose life and faith has been hammered out on the anvil of more challenges than many of us face. John and Lorraine possess a grace that doesn't burden you with their pain, but lifts you up in yours. That is a rare gift. Once you read this book, you'll understand just how special it is."

Reggie McNeal
Author, *The Present Future, Missional Renaissance:*
Changing the Scorecard for the Church
Missional Leadership Specialist, Leadership Network, Dallas, TX

"This book will help many discover hope and perspective in the midst of unexplainable crises. John and Lorraine Baergen explore their family's courageous journey towards a refined faith in God that brings courage for the future."

Dr. Keith Taylor
Lead Pastor
Beulah Alliance Church, Edmonton, AB

UNWRITTEN

There's still hope for your greater dream...

John and Lorraine Baergen

with Malcolm Petch

UNWRITTEN

ISBN: 978-1-77069-253-4

Printed in Canada

Word Alive Press
131 Cordite Road, Winnipeg, MB R3W 1S1
www.wordalivepress.ca

Library and Archives Canada Cataloguing in Publication

Baergen, John, 1944-

    Unwritten / John and Lorraine Baergen.

ISBN 978-1-77069-253-4

    1. Baergen, John, 1944-. 2. Baergen, Lorraine, 1947-.
    3. Traffic accident victims--Canada--Biography.

    I. Baergen, Lorraine, 1947- II. Title.

RD96.6.B34 2011   362.197'102800922   C2011-902674-0

DEDICATED TO:

The delight of our lives,
our grandsons, Sawyer, Mason, and Wyatt.
Through whom we have been given a second chance.

AND

To their parents, Brent and Sabrina.
For their commitment, together with us,
to influence their boys for Jesus!

Table of Contents

Foreword

When John and Lorraine first asked me about helping them with this project, I had no idea what I'd be getting into.

Frankly, I don't think they did, either.

Over this year and a half of working together, I've grown to know these two people very well. I've watched them wrestle with how transparent they should or shouldn't be with the deep and painful aspects of their story. Each time they've wrestled, I've watched them opt for openness when they could have chosen the safer route of self-protection. It's not easy to be as straightforward and honest as I've seen John and Lorraine be. They joke that I know things about them as individuals and as a couple that no one else knows. They allowed me and even encouraged me to ask probing questions about their innermost motivations and thoughts during some of the darkest days of their lives—and they didn't hold back from admitting the things that weren't pretty.

I've seen their courage lived out in front of me real-time—they went through unexpected and significant transition in both their professional and family lives, even while we were working on this book. The life of faith I see in John and Lorraine is not trapped in the past; they live it every day.

If you've never met the Baergens before, if you're just leafing through this book wondering whether or not there's anything in here for you, you might be wondering who they are as people outside of these pages. Let me share a small example of what I've observed in these two. Even though the focus of our times together was specifically for the purpose of writing about their journey, John and Lorraine made a point of always connecting with me on a personal level, showing genuine interest and concern for the things going on in my personal life, my business life, and even in my role as an elder at the church where I serve. They honestly cared about my family and me. That's different than what I've experienced in a lot of other projects I've worked on, and it says a great deal to me about who John and Lorraine are. These two are real people. Their journey is a real journey. Your unwritten tomorrows can truly be affected for the better by what John and Lorraine have shared in these pages.

No, I didn't know what I would be getting into when the Baergens asked me to help them with this project. I had no concept for the amount of uncharted territory we'd be covering together, but if I had known, I would still have said yes in a heartbeat. This has been an unexpected treasure for me, and my connection with John and Lorraine has now become a significant part of my own journey. I think you'll really benefit from their story—I know I have. I think you'll really like getting to know them—I know I have. And I think when you're finished reading this book and realize how tangible the Greater Dream can be for you, no matter what circumstance you find yourself in right now, you'll want to read more from John and Lorraine—I know I do!

Malcolm Petch
Kelowna, B.C.

Introduction

This is not a book of magic formulas to make your life successful. Neither is it a commentary on the crisis of the world around us and how it needs to be fixed.

What this book is, in essence, is a story—the story of our family, and its journey back from overwhelming tragedy. It's a story about rediscovering hope in the midst of crisis—hope that goes deeper than despair, further than faith. It's a story of hope that goes beyond hope, even in the face of God's seeming silence. And it's the story of rekindled hope in the Greater Dream—the dream we were all built for.

But this is not just our story—at least not exclusively.

If we were to recount our story simply for the sake of telling it, we wouldn't bother. It's too personal and too painful to walk through again just for the sake of getting it out there. We're telling our story because we've come to the conclusion that if God can use what we've walked through to help shed light on someone else's journey, then we're willing to revisit the pain again.

In that sense, this is our story. But in a deeper sense, what happened to us goes way beyond our story. We don't want it to be just our story. For most of us, much of our stories are still unwritten, and the insights we gain today help us shape the tomorrow we will end up living.

So, with that in mind, we want *Unwritten* to be *your* story. Or, to say it another way, *Unwritten* is intended to engage you where you are right now, and to invite you to walk the journey of your life through the chapters of our family's experience.

We hope and believe that during your time spent with us over the following pages you will find a reflection of things you've walked through on your own journey. Certainly the situations and circumstances will be different, but our deepest hope is that the heart lessons—the tough things we've had to live through, the mistakes we've made and the values we've embraced—will come to ring true in your own life, no matter where you are on the journey. Our prayer is that by the end of our story, you will find your own heart stirred again to believe that maybe, just maybe, the Greater Dream you were built for is still within your grasp.

You, too, know that there is something more... more than your present experience. We hear that every week from leaders we work with across the country. And we agree. Our invitation to you today is to consciously open your spirit up to God as you read, and to ask Him to shed light on your own journey through our story as shown on these pages.

When our lives were ripped apart on an icy highway on New Year's Day, we never thought we'd end up where we are today. But that's the beauty of life: the tomorrows are still uncharted territory; they're chapters in the book of life still waiting to be written. How the story unfolds is up to us. The pen rests in our hand as we set out to write the rest of the story.

So we invite you to turn the page and share life with us for a bit. Everything you and we have been through, every choice we've made, has brought us to where we are in this moment—and right now, this moment is all we have.

But tomorrow is still Unwritten.

With love,
Lorraine & John Baergen

CHAPTER 1

PARTY'S OVER

It was the sounds, I remember now, that first caught my attention and started pulling me out of the black void. The rattling wheels of the medical carts passing in the hallway, the muted bleeps from monitors and other medical equipment, the hushed voices uttering words I couldn't quite understand; bit by bit, the random pieces of information sifted their way into my consciousness.

I tried opening my eyes.

Bad move. It took every bit of strength in me to pry my eyelids apart. The resulting blast of light burned through my eyes and deep into my brain. All I could make out was a blur of colour and movement. There was no definition whatsoever in what I could see.

I rested again after the exertion. The void didn't seem so bad after all, and at least there was peace in the silence.

The sounds came again, but this time one of the voices seemed familiar. And because the person speaking was nearer to me, I understood his words.

"John, can you hear me? John, it's Jack."

Jack Klemke, a good friend. I knew that voice. I started to surface again.

"John, can you hear me? John, there's been a really bad car wreck. You've been in a bad car crash."

A car wreck? How could that be? I didn't remember anything like that.

"John, can you hear me?"

Through the fog, I thought I could feel Jack's hand holding mine. I focused and squeezed my fingers around his.

"John! Hey, my friend, it's good to have you back!" There was a distinct tone of relief in Jack's voice.

I tried clearing my head. What had happened to me? Where was Lorraine? Where were the boys? My eyes were still not cooperating and any movement I tried didn't feel very good. There seemed to be things sticking to every part of my body.

I settled back and tried to make sense of everything that was going on.

New Year's Day, 1981. That much I could remember.

After a fantastic Alberta-style family Christmas the week before, we took a seven-hour road trip to be with friends for New Year's Eve. We stopped along the way in Edmonton, about five hours from home, and bought each of our sons a new vest. Just a fun family outing over the Christmas break.

At our friends' home, my wife Lorraine and I spent many enjoyable hours catching up with them and simply hanging out. Our nine-year-old son, Byron, and his six-year-old brother, Brent, relished the chance to play with other children and to have fun with their still-new Christmas toys.

We rang in the New Year together and then tumbled off to bed. Morning would come early, and we were heading home the next day to get a jump on the week.

January 1 dawned a clear and fairly warm day for the middle of winter. When it came time to leave, we piled into the car for the seven-hour trip home. I remember the open sky lighting up the colourful scenery around us as we drove along the Alberta highway. The road was mostly bare and wet, due to the warmth of the sun in the clear sky. As we drove, the car was full of satisfaction and peace.

Around dinnertime, we passed through Whitecourt, a small town about halfway between Edmonton and our hometown, and hunted for a restaurant where we could take a break from the road and enjoy a nice meal. But because it was New Year's Day, all the eateries along the highway were closed. We settled for a full tank of gas and a few snacks from the gas station.

Evening had set in when we left Whitecourt and got back on the road. Brent and Byron giggled in the back seat, tugging back and forth at Byron's new electronic game and chatting about the things six- and nine-year-old brothers talk about. Brent always saw his big brother Byron as his larger-than-life hero, and the two of them loved spending time together—it certainly didn't matter to them that they'd been cooped up in the back seat of a car all day.

"Hey Dad," called Byron. "Tell us the bull story! Remember that time when you were a kid and the bull crashed through the corral gate? Tell us the story again—please!"

"Okay, Byron, I will!"

I remember glancing up at his happy face in the rear-view mirror.

Brent piped up, "Yeah, tell us again, Dad!"

And that's all I remembered. Just a typical family heading home from a good time with friends—enjoying each other's company and sharing stories about life growing up on a dairy farm.

And now I was here, trying desperately to emerge from the fog that enveloped me, trying to make sense of what my friend Jack had just told me.

There's no night-and-day cycle in a hospital's intensive care unit. The hustle and bustle is constant, a steady backdrop of sound and activity.

My reconnection to the world of the living took place gradually that first week. Initially, I didn't have times of sleeping and then being awake. Instead, I slipped in and out of the haze that constantly shrouded me. There were times I was more awake and lucid, and then times when the world again faded into nothingness.

And there were times when I was aware of my surroundings, but those around me must not have known I was "present," because I'd occasionally overhear healthcare workers talking about my condition—conversations they might not have had so close to my bed if they'd known I could hear them.

"Mr. and Mrs. Heidebrecht? I'm Dr. Swanson from Intensive Care." The doctor was speaking to Lorraine's parents. It sounded as though they were just outside the door. "Uhh, if you're wanting to see John alive, you'll need to go in really soon..." I remember feeling sorry for my in-laws, realizing they must be dealing with a lot.

Although I'd heard that same prognosis spoken other times in those first few days of awareness, it took me a while to realize that the doctors were actually referring to me. Obviously, they were not expecting me to live long. But despite the discouraging atmosphere around me, I felt a strong sense of peace and comfort developing inside; it felt like I was being held by a strength outside myself. I recognized that presence to be Jesus. I began to know at a deep level that the One to whom I had entrusted my life was now holding me. Peace, comfort, the feeling of being carried along almost like a child... that was the sustenance that enabled me to remain in this world, and to move forward in my quest to make sense of what was happening in those early days.

At that point, of course, I had no idea how radically my life had changed. I was coming to grips with the fact that something catastrophic had happened, but the sense of being held in the arms of Jesus kept me in a place of profound peace as parts of the puzzle began drifting into place.

That peace was there for me when I overheard doctors and nurses discussing things they probably didn't want me to know. The peace was also when I heard people saying things they definitely did want me to hear, like from one man who was part of our church back home. To this day I cannot figure out how he got into my room. Immediate family members had access, as well as our pastor and my friend Jack, but everyone else was barred because of my fragile condition. To slip in, this man would have had to evade the workers at the front desk, the nurses at the intensive care nursing station, and the doctors and nurses roaming the hallways.

I awoke to find him standing at the foot of my bed. While I knew who he was, we weren't friends. And although I couldn't see clearly, there seemed to be something strange about the way he was watching me.

"Hey, Baergen, I've just been in to see your son. He's not doing very well. In fact, I'd say he's not going to make it."

The man continued with what I remember as smugness and satisfaction.

"Baergen, your son looks bad. Really bad. I think he's going to die."

There was definitely spite and malevolence in his voice. It looked as though he was grinning at me, but it was definitely not out of compassion. He leaned in closer, staring me right in the eye.

"Baergen, you're not going to make it, either. You won't get out of here!"

With that final taunt, the man straightened up, turned, and strode out of the room.

I was stunned. I had no idea he hated me so much. I knew he was from my hometown, so when I realized he was standing at the foot of my bed I thought he was there to see how I was doing, or to bring messages of hope and support from friends. But this was no encouragement.

Our town was not that big, situated about five hours from the nearest big city. The discovery of oil and natural gas in the region in the late 1970s had increased the size of the city steadily, but with a population of just over 24,000 in 1981, it didn't take much to stand out in a crowd.

As established business people during the region's economic boom, Lorraine and I enjoyed a somewhat public profile due to our growing development company and mortgage brokerage firm. There were other reasons we were well known, but most of the recognition resulted from our business activities. At times we were called upon for media quotes when reporters were looking for a local comment on a business or economic story. We were happy with life as it was.

The news of our accident had caused quite a stir in the community when it broke in the local media on the morning of January 2—all unbeknownst to me, of course. One local radio announcer even stated on air that I'd been killed in the crash. But to paraphrase Mark Twain, "The news of my death had been greatly exaggerated."

Yet with the spotlight over the years came the occasional jealous swipe from others who perhaps felt we were getting too big for our britches. While it's not something you expect, it's still not surprising when it happens. It's the kind of thing you learn to live with.

But this, a person coming all the way to the city hospital to stand at the foot of my bed and deliver his brand of "encouragement"—this was something I'd never experienced before. I was floored by the intensity of his dislike for me and my family, and his almost gleeful reaction to our situation.

Still, the comfort of being held in the arms of Jesus carried me forward.

By the end of the week, I was pretty much back to full awareness—at least as much as I could be with all the medication being pumped into me. Everything was still blurry, but I could keep my eyes open and was able to acknowledge people when they spoke to me. The world around me started to make more sense, although I still struggled to understand exactly what had happened.

My friend Jack had been back in to see me several times, and he'd explained a few more details of the crash.

"You probably didn't even see it coming," Jack said. "From what the police can determine to this point, the other driver—in a three-quarter ton pick-up and pulling a trailer—lost control on the gradual corner you were just coming to. His trailer started swinging out, which pulled the back of his truck along with it, and the whole thing came down the road sideways right toward your vehicle as you drove over the crest of the rise."

I wasn't able to speak, but I sure had questions. I'm sure Jack could see them in my eyes.

"Yes, John, he was going too fast. The road was icing over, but even if he'd been on dry pavement the other driver was going far too fast."

I kept looking at Jack.

"Yes, John, the man had been drinking. It was New Year's Day, remember?"

It was amazing the way Jack anticipated my silent queries.

"No, he's not in the hospital here. From my understanding, he was hardly injured and went home after being treated in the emergency room."

Even in my medicated state I could feel a few things floating to the surface, one of which was relief that the crash had not been my fault. The other was a definite need to understand how something like this could happen— weren't we under God's protection?

It was a lot to absorb and process. Yet I still felt I was being held by Jesus, and I allowed myself to rest back into that place of comfort.

From my bed I could hear a man's voice repeatedly saying "No, no, no, no!" from somewhere across the room. I couldn't see who he was or what was happening, but even in my altered state I understood he was dealing with things too traumatic for him to handle.

"No, no, no, no, no!" As the voice continued, everything within me wanted to find out what was troubling him. I was still very much aware of being held in the arms of Jesus, and I knew this gentleman needed the peace I had.

"No, no, no, no!" Again the voice called. How I wished I could connect with him somehow, that I could share the restfulness and hope I had!

But it was not to be. His constant calling grew in intensity over the hours, and then, all of a sudden, faded. The silence afterward was sombre, and the atmosphere in the ward, which was far from encouraging to begin with, became very subdued for a while.

Days later, when I could speak a little, I motioned a nurse over to my bedside and asked about the man who'd been in the bed across from mine. She told me he'd actually been a doctor at the hospital, someone they'd all known and worked with. During my time across from him he was in the final stages of a terminal illness, and what I'd heard was his fear of dying, which was so strong that it had cracked sharply through his normal veneer of control and semi-arrogance.

I didn't know the full story at that time, of course. All I knew then was that this man was afraid and had no way of dealing with his fear.

A few days later, as I was resting, one of the nurses came into the room, checked my vital signs and the IV drip, and asked if I was comfortable. My jaw and facial bones were wired together, and because I couldn't express myself well if I needed anything, the staff constantly checked to make sure I was okay.

Just as she was about to leave my bedside, the nurse stopped and turned back to the head of my bed. Leaning over toward me, she looked me straight in the eyes.

"Are you a Christian?" she asked quietly but intently. I lifted my finger and beckoned her closer to me, because all I could do was whisper. She leaned in right close.

"Yes," I whispered through my wired-shut mouth. "Are you, too?"

She shook her head. "No, I'm not."

I beckoned her close again, and dug deep for enough strength to speak. "Why would you ask me that if you're not a Christian?"

She stepped back a bit, but still looked right at me. Her gaze was steady.

"I've worked on this ward for more than two years," she said quietly. "I've seen many people admitted during that time, and I've seen many pass away. You are the first person I've ever seen who is not afraid of death."

I didn't know what to say. Death certainly did seem like a possibility in those early days after the crash. The pain was intense—my facial bones were crushed, my skull and collarbone were fractured, cranial fluid was leaking from my nose, and my pelvis and hip were shattered. Given that I'd been hovering on the edge of death, her question intrigued me.

She looked at me again, patted my hand softly, then left the room to continue her duties.

I'd known all week the sense of being held in the arms of Jesus, but I hadn't realized until that moment how His peace, so active in me, was also apparent to others observing me. I closed my eyes and rested in that reality.

Looking back, I have no doubt that His love, that sense of being held by Jesus, is what carried me through.

What I didn't know back then—and it was good that I didn't know—was that the week I'd just lived through would be the easiest week I'd face for a long, long time.

*   *   *   *

I had a very different experience from John in that first week after the crash.

The first thing I remember is regaining consciousness while sitting on the highway. The pavement under me was icy cold, but I wasn't aware enough to grasp that something was wrong. I must have kept drifting back into unconsciousness, because I recall there being several times when I sort of woke up and wondered again what was going on.

Everything was quiet.

When you're driving, the constant low hum of the engine and the gentle moan of tires on pavement become part of the soundscape; they're always there, and the sounds all blend together to form the road trip soundtrack. They fade into the background.

But when the sounds stop, the silence becomes very loud.

I drifted back again. This time I noticed tiny shards of smashed windshield all around me on the pavement. I had no idea what these sparkling little pieces of glass were, nor did I understand what the implications of their presence were for me or my family.

Again, I drifted back, still on the highway. It seemed there were some sounds, after all, which stood out in the stillness. I could hear a faint metallic ticking from behind me somewhere, caused by the hot engine block from our car cooling rapidly in the winter air. Again, I had no idea what the sound was or what it meant out here in the middle of nowhere.

The next time I drifted awake, I heard approaching sirens, which after a period of getting louder suddenly stopped. Then there were slamming vehicle doors and the approaching footsteps and efficient voices of a crew of paramedics.

Someone came up to me, shone a flashlight in my face, and started talking. I had no idea what he was saying or what he was asking. Strong hands helped me up off the ground and led me to an ambulance, where I was directed to sit in the front passenger seat.

I still had no idea what had happened, or what was going on around me, and I made no effort to figure it out. I just sat there, drifting in and out, while this blur of activity continued.

Had I been conscious, I would have heard a loud noise like a chainsaw. We didn't know it until much later, but this was the inaugural run for the town of Whitecourt's new "Jaws of Life," a device built to extricate people trapped in wrecked cars. Just before Christmas, about a week before we arrived, the town had purchased the unit—and now already there was a desperate need for it to be put to use. I wasn't even aware of the noise, but the Jaws of Life were ripping into our Cadillac to free John and Byron, who were trapped in the wreckage. I'm glad that at the time I didn't realize what was happening.

Then we were moving. As my ambulance raced down the highway back toward the town of Whitecourt, I found myself thinking, *Wow, this guy needs to slow down. If he keeps going this fast we could have an accident!* I was in such a state of shock that I had no comprehension of what was happening.

I must have drifted off again, because when I awoke I found myself lying on a stretcher in what appeared to be a gleaming white hallway. When I turned my head to one side, I saw another stretcher beside mine—and there was someone on it. I tried hard to see who it was, and then realized it was my son Brent.

I slowly turned my head to the other side, and recognized Byron lying on his own stretcher. By this time I knew something terrible had happened, but was reassured to see both my sons were still alive and with me.

John!

Adrenaline shot through me as I realized I couldn't see my husband.

"Please, someone," I called out. "Can anyone tell me where my husband is?"

Someone in a white lab coat approached. "Hello, Mrs. Baergen. Your husband is here, too. He's in a room down the hallway."

I remember being reassured by that; my sons were beside me where I could see them, and John was with us here, too, although in another room.

I remained awake, although groggily so, and was eventually wheeled into my own room. I'd closed my eyes to rest when I heard a quiet conversation just beyond my bed.

"We're going to have to put her out for that, of course," said one voice. Another voice replied, but I wasn't able to hear the answer.

Put her out? Was that me they were talking about? What did they mean by that?

Later I learned that the conversation was about my face, which had suffered severe lacerations in the crash. They did put me out, like they'd said, and the only doctor available that night—a young intern serving on-call in the emergency room at this tiny little rural hospital—sewed my face back together, using eighty-four stitches in the process. What damage a forceful exit through the windshield can cause!

More than my appearance was going to change, of course, in the coming days, weeks, and months. Like John, I was completely unaware of how significantly everything I knew had been shattered and uprooted forever because of that swift and devastating moment on an icy highway.

When I awoke the next morning, I was told that John and Byron had been airlifted to a larger hospital in Edmonton where they'd each receive better care for their extensive, life-threatening injuries.

Brent had also been transported to the same larger hospital. He'd suffered an extremely long laceration, one that ran from his forehead all the way back across his head. His leg was also badly broken just below the hip, so he'd been put in traction. But even with these injuries, I was told Brent was in the best shape of the three of them.

John was critically injured—there really was no hope for his survival in those early days. All I could do was pray for him as the reports came back to me day by day.

When hospital staff finally felt they could tell me about Byron, I learned that he was in a coma. The doctors told me that Byron was almost certainly brain-injured and that his condition would have long-term implications for our family.

Brain-injured.

I'd trained as a registered nurse and could usually understand medical terms and treatments, but I had no real comprehension of what the term "brain-injured" meant. For someone else, I could have seen the fuller context and understood—but when it was my own son in question, I simply could not fathom all that was meant by this traumatic and rather terrifying report.

My own injuries—the facial lacerations and four broken ribs—now seemed fairly minor, at least compared to the rest of my family. I was told I'd remain in the little town hospital to begin my healing process.

Thankfully, my sister Carol came to be with me in Whitecourt. Steady, strong, and focused, Carol had always been able to grasp situations quickly and respond appropriately. She came with other family members the day after the crash, and when John and the boys were sent off to Edmonton to get the help they needed Carol stayed with me and took charge of my recovery.

Other family members and friends started popping by, too. Most of them visited with me briefly on their way to the city to visit John and the boys. Some, however, made time to sit and talk. Often our conversations focused on what God might be up to in the whole situation—I had an unshakeable belief that Jesus would heal Byron, and I had a very strong sense that He could use everything we were dealing with for the greater good.

"Do you think God was trying to get your attention?" our pastor asked. We'd been talking about some of the events in our lives as a couple in the months leading up to the crash.

I'd never thought about that. When I pondered our lives to that point, being as objective as possible, I saw we'd always genuinely tried to live out our faith in the community, working in ways that could truly help others on their own spiritual journeys. We were committed and intentional about pursuing the deeper things in life.

"No," I mused, "I don't think He was trying to get our attention; I think He's had our attention for some time. But I do think He's been taking us deeper, shaping and moulding our character even more."

And He really *had* been shaping us, both spiritually and in other ways. That was going to become a lot clearer to both of us in the months ahead.

At that moment, though, there in that little hospital in Whitecourt, my focus was narrowing toward an immediate goal: I really wanted to get to the city to be with my family.

"Mrs. Baergen, you have a phone call," said a nurse coming in from the hallway.

Phone calls had been a regular staple for me, sometimes up to three a day, as doctors from the metropolitan hospital called with updates about John and our two sons. Edmonton was only a two-hour drive away, but my desire to be with my family was so strong that it seemed like they were on another continent.

There was no phone in my room, so Carol usually took my calls at the nurses' station.

"It was Jack Klemke," Carol said on her return to the room. "He wanted to know how you're doing." Jack and his wife—her name was also Carol—were good friends of ours, yet I was surprised it was Jack on the phone and not the doctor whose call I had expected.

"What did you tell him?" I asked, wincing a bit as I spoke. The stitches on my face were swelling and starting to leak. I wasn't much in the mood for looking in the mirror that week.

"I told him you're on the mend, at least as far as your ribs are concerned. I didn't mention your face; it hasn't changed in the last couple of days."

"Did he see John today?" I asked. Jack lived in the city, and he had been visiting John regularly.

"That's mainly why he called. He knows you want to get there quickly, and he has a proposal for us to consider. When the doctors here discharge you, Jack wants you to call him immediately. He'll send his private plane to get us, and then we'll both fly to Edmonton so you can be with John as soon as possible."

I was thrilled! All I wanted was to be with my family, and the wait was unbearable. Here, though, was a workable solution. Jack's plane would make short work of the distance, and at that point I much preferred the thought of a quick, smooth flight to a long, bumpy car ride.

Carol left to discuss details with Jack, and I settled down in my bed, feeling a little more hopeful. It was very touching to have other people look out for me. Jack and his wife were friends, and I could tell this was one of the ways they felt they could best help us.

My sister had been a lifesaver, too. We'd trained together as nurses, and while I'd changed course to become John's wife and business partner, she'd left nursing to join a world mission agency. Carol had accepted an agency posting in Vienna, Austria, and had actually been scheduled to fly there during the first weeks of January. When she received news of our crash, she called Vienna and postponed her move for at least a month. That demonstration of her commitment to us was amazing and deeply valued.

Finally, near the end of the week, I was told I was well enough to travel. Carol phoned Jack with the news, and Jack, in turn, sent his crew to prepare for the short flight.

But the plane trip was not to be. A blizzard rolled in that morning, and after three attempts to land, the pilot aborted his flight plan and headed back with an empty plane.

And I was left feeling empty, too. All I wanted was to reunite with my family.

Again, my competent and determined sister came to the rescue. She collected me and my stuff and gallantly rode with me on the Greyhound bus from small-town Whitecourt all the way to Edmonton.

I wanted to go to my family, yes, but I hadn't planned on going by bus. I longed to talk with John again as quickly as possible, but I dreaded the two-hour bus trip. The last thing I wanted was to be seen in public—the swelling around the stitches was worse than ever, and had reached the point where my face was literally leaking.

But since the bus was my only option, I pulled myself together, sat myself as far away from everyone else as possible, and kept my face turned toward the window. As the miles passed, I became preoccupied with preparing myself for what I would see when I finally arrived in Edmonton.

I couldn't help but notice familiar scenery as the bus pulled out of White-court and headed down the highway toward the city. Seven days earlier my family and I had been on this same road, laughing together and enjoying family stories. One week ago it was a new year, life was good, and we were happy.

How drastically everything had changed in those seven days.

There wasn't much I could do to hide the tears slipping down my face. I stared out the window and found myself wondering if this was what people meant by "hitting bottom." Was this what the bottom looked like for us?

Looking back, I can say that the trip to the city hospital was the lowest point of my life. Technically, I was no longer in shock, but I was still reeling from the impact of all that had happened. I mean, who among us ever plans for these sudden turns in the journey of life? Certainly, we'd purchased car insurance and life insurance, but we'd bought those policies because it was the right thing to do, not because we were planning for bad things to happen to us. Insurance policies can offer financial, economic "protection"—after all, a car can be replaced—but they offer absolutely no protection from the real-life results of a split-second event on an icy highway.

At Christmas and on New Year's Eve, life had been wonderful. Now, a week later, it was like the pause button had been pushed on all our plans and dreams. Life had been pulled in around us, from the big picture down to an intense focus on the here and now. I was scrambling to find something—any-thing—I could cling to for hope.

I'd never been in this place before. I'd never even *thought* about being in this place before. The life experience I'd gained and the work God had done in grooming my character now converged with great intensity in my present experience. I couldn't see the way forward, but I had no choice except to keep going, even if it was inch by inch.

If I knew anything for certain, it was that what I had considered "normal" was over. Now, a New Normal had to be created.

I was discovering some fundamental truths about myself. Preparation for this unwritten portion of my life—whether I was aware of it or not—was finished. Whatever foundations had been built into my life were now all I had to stand on. There was no opportunity to go back and rewrite my life experiences; whatever I'd allowed God to do in me up to that point was all I had to build on as I moved forward.

I couldn't articulate it clearly at the time, though. Sitting on that bus, heading to Edmonton, all I knew was that a door had closed on the first part of our lives. I knew a new door was opening, but I had absolutely no idea what lay across the threshold.

Staring out the window of that cranky old Greyhound, it seemed to me that I was in way over my head. What awaited me at the city hospital? It was one thing to get updates over the phone—but what would it be like when I actually saw John, Byron, and Brent? I was relieved to finally be on my way to be with John and the boys, but I had to admit there was a bit of fear still tugging at my heart.

Everything was different now.

This was absolutely the lowest point in my life—of that much, I was sure. But certainly things would start to improve now, right? That was the fear I hesitated to voice, 'Things couldn't actually get worse, could they?'

That's what I was about to discover.

Musings

CHAPTER 2

DREAMS REMEMBERED

In the animated movie *Robots*, Ewan McGregor's character Rodney leaves home to pursue his dream of being an inventor. Inspired by the legendary robotic innovator BigWeld, Rodney is spurred on toward greatness by his father, who had dreams of his own to be a musician but settled for life as a dishwasher. Rodney's hopes are dashed when he reaches the big city and finds things are not as he'd envisioned. He faces a crisis of soul and relationship as he wrestles with the decision to either keep his dream alive or to give up and go home.

In the true-to-life movie *The Rookie*, Dennis Quaid plays family man Jimmy Morris—a teacher at a small-town high school and coach of the school's baseball team. Jimmy has given up on his dream of playing in the major leagues. Early in the film we see him as a young man and learn that his remarkable talent for pitching was strongly downplayed by his father and sidelined by his father's military career. Despite the lack of support and encouragement, Jimmy keeps improving his ball-playing skills throughout high school and becomes a major league draft pick, only to have an arm injury permanently derail his hopes without him ever having played a single game. Years later, when the high school team he coaches challenges him to attend tryouts with some pro scouts, Jimmy has to deal with his neutralizing thought patterns and long-held belief systems—including facing his father—before he can even start believing that maybe his dream is not dead after all.

For Lorraine and me, our understanding of what living the Greater Dream meant for us became clear fairly early in our marriage. Although it wasn't fully realized yet, we could have summarized what was important to us and, to a large extent, why we were doing what we were doing in life.

We also knew we didn't want to settle for the "same old, same old" we saw around us. We didn't want to settle for a lesser life; we sensed we were made for something more, both as individuals and as a couple, and we were determined to pursue it, whatever "it" was.

I believe it's that way for many of us. The realization often comes when we're lying in bed dreading the next day at work, speculating how we ever got to where we are and wondering if there's anything we can do about it. Or it hits when we suddenly remember the joy we found in the simplest of things as a kid, and we mourn the loss of that. For some of us, realization comes through a jolt that suddenly opens our eyes to what's real and meaningful in our lives.

That's how it was for me.

As a young husband, and fairly new in my commitment to Jesus, I was happy with where my life was going—I had a great wife, a stable life, and enough financial freedom to explore and pursue new business opportunities.

I was far from perfect, of course, but I would have considered myself a normal guy. I was dealing with the stuff that most other normal guys deal with. I was focused on trying to live a good and honest life—keeping my ego in check, staying true to my wife, being a good dad, and living with integrity.

I had a friend back then named Lionel. He was older than I was, maybe even fifteen or twenty years older, but we really connected well. We met regularly to talk about life and finances and other things. I got to know him through his job as a grain buyer, but as our friendship grew our common interests drifted into other areas as well. Usually when we met he'd ask where I thought he should invest or not invest; I became kind of a novice financial advisor to him.

I can remember specifically when I was struck by the realization that there had to be something more. Lionel and I had met for coffee as we usually did, and for the most part our conversation was typical of the other times we'd chatted. Right at the end, almost as we were going out the door of the coffee shop, Lionel mentioned he was going in for surgery the next week.

"I gotta admit, John, that I'm more than a little nervous about this surgery thing," Lionel told me. "They tell me it's just exploratory, but I'm thinking maybe it's more serious than the doctor is saying." He chuckled nervously. "I've never been under general anaesthetic before."

I grinned and slapped his shoulder. "Hey, buddy, you're a strong dude," I told him, brushing off his concern. "You're tough—you'll be fine. The doctors won't find anything wrong with you. Just wait and see!"

Lionel smiled, and as we exited the café we talked about when we could next get together.

I was in my home office the next week when I got the phone call. Lionel had died on the operating table with virtually no warning.

I instantly went weak in the knees. Our last conversation rushed back at me, and I could hear the fear in his words as he spoke of the surgery. Why hadn't I listened?

I was floored by the tragedy of his death at a young age, and even more so by my failure to adequately respond to his concerns. I could have taken the time to hear his heart, and maybe even pray with him, but I let my lack of spiritual intentionality cut the conversation short. He'd reached out to me in his time of crisis. Even though I had some awareness of the deeper things of life, and could have shared part of my own faith journey with him, I chose instead to offer only light-hearted encouragement, which meant nothing.

That's when I made a determined decision to pursue the deeper things in life, to let my life stand for something meaningful. Until that point, I'd let my growing awareness of God bring more intentionality to me only as a husband and businessman. After the tragedy with Lionel, though, I became focused and purposeful about looking beyond myself, speaking the truth I knew, and letting my life make a difference beyond ethics and good business practices.

Lorraine, in her way, had already been gently pulling me toward living the Greater Dream, but with my single-mindedness God had needed to use a significant blow to get my attention. Lionel's death was that blow—now I was listening.

Lorraine and I had heard that a prominent evangelist was coming to a town within driving distance of us, and I felt compelled to connect with him to see if we could help within his ministry in some way. We established a social connection, and when his local mission was wrapped up we agreed to go fishing a couple hundred miles into the middle of nowhere.

I do not really enjoy fishing, although I gravitate toward a more rugged life. Heading into the outdoors always appeals to me. I like to get my hands dirty and know the feel of the earth in my fingers, so to speak. Sitting on a boat, enjoying the clean air—that is good. But trying to figure out where the fish are biting, what depth they're at, which lure is going to attract them best, I've never really wanted to figure that out. I was willing to endure it all, though, because I knew fishing meant a great deal to this man. So, for the purpose of being with someone I viewed as significant in guiding me on my journey, this trip seemed well worth the investment.

Lorraine supported this quest to find greater direction and meaning for our lives. In this instance, that meant she willingly travelled to this remote town and stayed with Byron in a tiny hotel room while I went fishing.

As we floated around, I spoke about some of the things I'd been pondering since Lionel's death. I wondered aloud how I could connect with someone like him in ministry and also make a difference in people's lives. I spoke from the deepest places of my heart. I asked what I thought were pertinent questions. The evangelist, though, seemed more interested in talking about what I was doing in business.

After a while, he turned to me and spoke frankly. "Baergen, I just don't think you've got what it takes to be a spiritual leader."

I was stunned, to say the least.

"I think the best thing you could do is go home, make money, and just send it to me. That's where you could make the greatest impact for the ministry."

I stumbled through the rest of our time together in a daze. I'd really looked up to this man, and now he was telling me I didn't have what it takes to tackle the more meaningful things I believed I was being called toward.

When we finally packed up our gear and headed back toward civilization, it was pretty silent in the cab of the pick-up. I didn't know if this man knew how deeply he'd misunderstood me, and how completely he'd disempowered me, but frankly I didn't care. The truth is, I don't think he cared, either!

This man was known for having a strong impact on people through his effective communication, but his credibility and ability to speak into my life had plummeted in my eyes. He had failed to grasp what was really going on inside me. He'd basically said I was a big zero, a man with no gifts, with no meaningful place in life other than to make money to support people like him. But on that long and silent drive back to the hotel, in the deepest part of me I would not accept that I was a big zero. I just could not believe that.

I formed a quiet resolve to shake off this man's evaluation and just dig in and "do life." I'd keep moving forward with the things that were important to us, and I'd keep pushing on the doors in front of me. I wasn't about to send this particular evangelist any of my money, either.

Had I known then what I know now, I would have realized I was on a quest to find a mentor. I was searching for someone with more life experience in the things that mattered to me, someone who grasped the bigger things and could help me unpackage them. I was looking for a man who could feed wisdom into my life in ways that would help refine me and move me along the life path I was walking.

After my behind-the-scenes experience with this well-known evangelist, I kept my cards a little closer to my chest, at least in my pursuit of finding someone older and wiser to speak into my dreams. I continued to expand my business pursuits, and Lorraine and I moved forward with building our family and walking out the Greater Dream, as best we understood it then, of having an impact on the spiritual pursuits of others.

We continued getting to know people, and spoke regularly about faith issues. I knew I was built to influence people on a spiritual level, and I was focused on keeping that pursuit forefront in my life.

One day I had a flash of brilliance—or so I thought.

Chuck Colson!

The idea intrigued me—it was definitely worth pursuing! Lorraine and I would get Colson to come up to Alberta, line up a couple of speaking engagements for him, and through his story get a bunch of our friends hooked on living with greater intentionality!

I was young, energetic, bursting with enthusiasm for all I could accomplish in the business world and for God, and I was ready to take on the giants!

Charles Colson was a significant mover and shaker in the Christian world in the mid- to late- 1970s. As one of the inner posse in Richard Nixon's infamous Watergate scandal, he was one of the few involved who actually went to jail. The experience revolutionized Colson's life in more ways than one; he'd become a follower of Jesus partway through the ordeal, introduced to Jesus by one of his highly-placed business friends about the same time he was sentenced to prison. His time behind bars revealed many things about life in the prison system that an outsider would probably never have noticed—and Colson couldn't walk away from what he'd learned. After he was released, pardoned by Gerald Ford, Colson went on to start a ministry called Prison Fellowship, which he leads to this day.

A brilliant researcher and scholar, Colson wrote a biography of his experience in Watergate and prison. It was powerful stuff. I remember reading it all the way through and loving every word. I must have given away caseloads of the book over the years to my friends and acquaintances in the business world.

I recall being hesitant about the cover of the book, though, because in big yellow letters it proclaimed the title—*Born Again!* Introducing people to Jesus was my whole purpose in giving the book away, of course, so I wasn't at all ashamed about Colson's choice of words. I just didn't want people to be put off by the title before they'd actually had a chance to read the book for themselves (the whole "you can't judge a book by its cover" deal). I got around that by dropping the book into a brown paper bag before giving it to someone with whom I'd already had introductory spiritual conversations. I'd say: "Read this, and then we'll talk!"

Colson's story impacted people, especially hardcore business people who weren't impressed by much. A number of my friends moved several steps closer to knowing Jesus after reading *Born Again!*

Lorraine and I had come up with the idea of hosting a large summer barbecue. Lorraine was involved in the Christian Women's Association, and I was always talking to business associates or handing out Colson's book, so we each interacted with a large group of upwardly mobile people. We wanted to throw a party that would be worth coming to, a warm-weather outdoor extravaganza that would draw people from the business community. Part of our plan was to feature a good speaker—and of course we wanted that speaker to be someone who could effectively communicate his or her personal faith journey with our business friends.

That's why the idea of having Colson as the speaker at our inaugural barbecue intrigued me so much. He was in high demand, was a superb communicator, and definitely had the life experience to capture the attention of our prospective guests.

More than that, we had a connection to Colson. We had a connection to Washington, D.C., anyway. My sister lived in the Washington area—or "Warshing-tun," as she called it—having married Don, a young engineer with the U.S. government's oceanographic division, NOAA. I felt I knew Don well enough to ask him for a favour.

"You want me to do what?" Don asked incredulously when I spoke with him on the phone.

"I'd like you to call Colson's office and see if you can arrange a meeting with him for me."

There was silence on the other end of the line for a couple of moments.

"Okay, John, I'll give it a whirl. But no promises—they don't know me from a hole in the ground, and I have no idea whether I'll be able to convince them to meet with you."

"That's good enough for me, Don," I said. "Just give it your best shot!"

A week later, Don phoned back. "It's done; it's all set. You're going to meet Colson for lunch."

I was ecstatic—our plans were coming together! We knew Colson was the right person to bring to Canada for the first of our barbecues.

We flew to Washington, D.C. and stayed with my sister. When the day of the lunch appointment arrived, my brother-in-law took the day off work and the two of us headed into the city.

The lunch was to be held at the Christian Embassy in Washington, D.C. The place was a constant hub of activity, with people coming and going from all over the globe.

Don and I were greeted and led into the dining room. The room itself was huge; the focal point was a massive solid oak table. Already seated around the table were several other guests dressed in ethnic clothing. It was obvious this wouldn't be an intimate lunch meeting, but I was still enthusiastic.

As we were seated, we were told that Colson and his wife had unexpectedly been called out of the city that morning due to a sudden family health crisis.

"Mr. Colson sends his regrets that he cannot meet with you personally, but he has sent his director in his place," explained the Prison Fellowship staff person. "Please enjoy your lunch with the director, and rest assured that any request you have come with will be treated as though Mr. Colson himself were meeting with you."

I was disappointed to not be meeting Colson himself, but as I had just lost my own father rather suddenly to a heart attack, I knew that circumstances in life could change abruptly. I settled in, ready to enjoy my lunch with the director and present my proposal as passionately as I could.

Colson's director came and joined us at the table, and Don and I were honoured to find we'd been seated next to him. It was to be a more personal meeting after all, despite the number of people at the table. I was encouraged.

We chatted through lunch about various things, enjoying conversations with many of the people who were in Washington from around the world. The director himself was a very large man, a confident ex-FBI agent still sporting a well-muscled frame. He had a very commanding presence and a deep, clear voice that filled the room when he spoke. I could see that Colson surrounded himself with good people.

Lunch finally drew to a close, and as our last cup of coffee was poured the director turned to me and said, "John, you're here from Canada, right?"

"Yes, I am."

"Well, why are you here? What would you like from us?"

I was energized, pumped to be finally making my presentation.

"Well, sir, my wife and I are planning to host barbecues for people who are exploring faith. I'd like to invite Mr. Colson to Canada to speak at one of these meetings—to tell his story and to communicate how his faith is making a difference in his life."

I felt the director's eyes bore into me. "John," he said, "how many hours of Bible study and prayer do you do each day?"

I froze in my seat, my eyes wide open and my hopeful smile still pasted on my face. This was something Lorraine had been talking with me about. She'd grown up in a home where Bible study and reflection were routine, but they certainly weren't part of my daily schedule. While Lorraine was concerned that I had no plans to deepen my grounding on spiritual matters, I continually brushed her off with comments about being too busy talking with others about my faith to spend much time reading the Bible. Had I been asked for a summary, I would have told Lorraine, "I'll talk, you read."

And now Colson's director had pulled this end-run on me.

The room went deathly quiet. I was sure everyone could hear my thumping heart as they awaited an answer from this Canadian spiritual giant.

I was frantic. I could feel my ambitions losing their grasp on the edge of the roof and beginning to tumble.I was tempted to lie, to make up some fantastic number to convince Colson's director I had spiritual substance. But his ex-FBI-agent eyes were still drilling into me, and I knew I'd never be able to pull it off. So I scrambled to add up every possible minute that could count toward Bible reading and prayer. I led an adult Bible class at the church, but we were a small group and I did it on the fly; not much preparation time went into it. But I did pray before every meal, at church, and sometimes with friends or my boys. I managed to nail down a number, although it was stretched so thin I knew it was transparent.

"Uhh, about thirty or forty minutes," I mumbled.

His ex-FBI face never moved a muscle. "John, when you're through playing spiritual games, call us."

I just listened, my eyes riveted to the floor.

"Colson is very busy, and the calls that come to us here are life-change serious," Colson's director said. "So as we prioritize where we're going to go, I'd say you're not ready for us at all."

And with that, the meeting was over. I didn't want to move. I didn't want to turn and look at anyone. I fervently wished that someone had thought to build a trap door under my chair I could just disappear into. Sliding out of view became my new number one priority—and it wasn't working. The only thing I was glad for was that Charles Colson himself had not been at the meeting.

Don and I endured the ride back to his home in Bethesda, Maryland in absolute silence. I don't think we exchanged more than a word or two the entire time.

That experience became a defining moment for me. The Colson event stands out in my mind as being a pivotal turning point in my spiritual walk. I'm sure God was preparing me for the dependence on Him I'd need to survive our car wreck and the years that followed. He was building the foundation I'd need to truly live the Greater Dream. I realize now that God needed someone with Colson's stature to get my attention. Anything less than the public challenge wouldn't have delivered the two-by-four blow needed to make me stop and truly listen.

The trip to Washington continued the shift in my priorities that had started with Lionel's death. I was still full of energy, still working hard at business, but I was beginning to let Jesus shape a lot more of my calendar, my agenda, and my very thinking.

A few years after that trip, the Canadian evangelist Terry Winter was preparing for a crusade in our hometown. The concept intrigued us. Although the mass meeting approach was not our way of introducing friends to spiritual matters, the support he was receiving from the whole community demonstrated a degree of unity at work. And unity is good; we agreed with that.

I was asked to be on the steering committee for the public meetings, but I declined. This was "canned Christianity," from my perspective, and it was neither up my alley nor something I was comfortable endorsing. Even though my fishing trip debacle had come and gone sometime earlier, I was still uneasy about connecting with a similar spiritual professional.

I hadn't planned to attend the crusade, but Lorraine's dad encouraged me to check it out before writing it off. So, with no expectations, I went with Lorraine to one of the early organizational meetings in hopes of meeting Winter.

For some reason, we felt an automatic connection with Terry. He was a fairly soft–spoken guy, yet very engaging, and Lorraine and I quickly came to respect him. In distinct contrast to the evangelist with whom we'd first interacted, Lorraine said she always felt Terry treated her as someone of significance, despite his high public profile. I appreciated his authenticity.

Despite the mass evangelism feel of the event, we decided to check out the crusade on the first night. I was pleasantly surprised at the straightforward way Terry addressed the crowd, and I realized that I'd been too hasty in writing off large meetings. The crusade lasted seven nights, and after our first night we got on the phone and started inviting our friends to attend

with us. In the end, we attended each of the next six evenings with a different couple from the business community. We were eager for our friends to
meet Terry and experience this relevant expression of faith. When we spoke
to Terry again after the crusade, he told us he'd been intrigued by how we'd
shown up with a different couple each night.

Unlike Lorraine, I'd only been a committed Christ follower for a short
time. While the Colson experience had forced me to re-establish my priorities, most of my growth in faith to that point had been self-initiated. In Terry
I'd found someone I respected, and someone who could impart a great deal
to me. He was as far on the other end of the spectrum as one could get from
the earlier evangelist I'd met, and Terry became my first mentor in the ways
of faith for the next few years.

When the crusade ended, Lorraine and I started talking about how to
engage our friends in a further journey of faith.

"What do we do?" asked Lorraine. "We can't just drop this conversation
now that the crusade is over."

I knew she was right. We gathered our friends who'd come with us to
the events and started a discussion group in our home on spiritual matters.
Having learned by experience the limited effectiveness of my on-the-fly style
of study, we elected to use materials prepared by a national parachurch organization. Some members of our family were involved with this organization, and a lot of its material was very good. The group study materials took
us through the basics of faith, and the last session culminated in a lesson on
putting our faith into action by telling others about it.

"I don't know, Lorraine," I said to her one day when we were planning for
our next study night. "I think the ideas the material is suggesting for telling
others about our faith are too mundane, too canned. Can't we do something
that feels more like us?"

"Let's check with the group," said Lorraine.

Not everyone in the group had even embraced faith in Jesus, so I was intrigued by what they might say when we talked about this lesson. When we
gathered again the next week as a group, we tossed around ideas for how to

take the next growth step, and the idea for summer barbecues was revisited. Everyone in the group loved the idea. I was enthusiastic and felt this was something I could really get behind.

When it was time to choose our first speaker, it seemed natural for us to invite Terry, as he'd been instrumental in introducing faith to all our group members.

This was a new adventure for us, and we all really enjoyed it. Yes, it was a lot of work, too. As I was growing more dependent on God, I was also growing out of my tendency to do everything myself and starting to see the team God was putting in place. Each group member helped organize the event, and Lorraine's family came alongside to help serve food and clean up. It was definitely a community event by the time it all came together. We learned a lot, too, about casting a compelling vision and then mobilizing a team around that vision.

We had a fairly large deck on the back of our house, overlooking a lake, and we thought it would be a great setting for the barbecue. A number of church friends heard what we were up to and asked about coming. We wanted the whole thing to be a community event more than a church gathering, so we told them they could come only if they invited people to attend with them who were honestly exploring faith issues.

The weather on the day of the barbecue was great, and the feeling of being on the right track was even better. We had a total of sixty-four people, and of those about half were still investigating faith. After Terry spoke, we were astonished at the number of people who decided to stake their faith on Jesus. The barbeque truly became a life-changing event for many who were there, and we were privileged to play a part!

After the barbecue, so many people wanted to explore their faith more deeply that a number of other discussion groups were launched. By the next summer, our original small group decided it wanted to host two separate barbecues, one at the start of the summer in June and another in August before the fall chill set in. We had a large workshop on the property, so if the weather turned nasty we could head for shelter and still be together as a group. We ended up having to expand our deck, just to be able to accommodate all the people. In fact, that became a normal routine for the next few years: host a barbecue, build the deck larger, host a bigger barbecue, expand the deck some more. By the third year, we had two hundred people seated at tables on our deck.

Terry spoke at six of these barbecues, and after that strong start we brought in other speakers, the best we could find from around North America. All I'd envisioned for these barbecues prior to our trip to see Colson was now becoming reality. As word spread, people we didn't even know—business people and others who lived their lives without any real knowledge of God—readily accepted our invitations.

And Terry was really helping me grow in my faith. After our initial connection, we maintained a good relationship, and he eventually started inviting us to teach Christian Life seminars with him in different communities across the country. I was excited to share my journey, but I was also thankful to have a person with Terry's faith and integrity to speak into my life and help me grow spiritually. His investment in me paved the way for a depth of faith I didn't know I'd need.

One of the offshoots from the growing impact of our small groups' barbecues was an increasing visibility in the community for both Lorraine and me. People in church circles already knew us, and now people in the community were starting to know who we were as well. It was affirming but also challenging for me to have a reporter call up and ask for a statement about how some national event was going to affect our economy here at home, but I realized that I would have to maintain a very high diligence in my business dealings as a publicly recognized follower of Jesus.

As leaders in our local church, Lorraine and I began to muse about hosting an appreciation service for members of the local Royal Canadian Mounted Police detachment, as a means of expressing our corporate thanks for their presence and work in our community. I suppose we could have shrugged it off as merely a good thought, but in our commitment to the Greater Dream we decided to explore the idea.

To ensure remote regions of the country have good police services, young RCMP recruits are usually stationed in several different outlying jurisdictions in their early years on the force. Away from their families and friends, they often have no real connection to the communities they serve.

Once the idea of expressing appreciation to the RCMP had sparked for us as a church, we were eager to press forward with it. We spoke to the RCMP superintendent, explained our intention, and invited him and his contingent to attend the service. And they did! About twenty-eight members of the force attended, and each one sat with a sponsoring couple from the church.

It was a wonderful and very colourful experience, as all the officers wore red serge uniforms. They entered the auditorium in formation, very formally, and the effect was rather awe-inspiring. The front page of the next day's paper even featured a shot of the officers in their dress uniforms lined up inside the church.

God knew what He was doing in me, too, and not just in the members of the local police force. I'd thought His idea was merely to let the RCMP members know that we, as a church, appreciated their hard work and service. But later I realized He was still shaping me spiritually, helping me grow more into living the Greater Dream.

After our crash, once I improved enough to be back in the community, I would run into someone every once in a while who knew who I was through having attended one of the barbecues, or through our connection with the RCMP appreciation service, and so on. They'd ask very probing questions about my faith and what I still believed in light of all that had happened to our family. Each time I would be forced to delve back into the Bible, longing to hear Jesus speak. How could I better share what I believed?

Even when I thought I was simply "giving back," God was leading me deeper and deeper into dependence on Him.

*　*　*　*

John is right when he talks about us living in pursuit of the Greater Dream. I could also have described it as "not settling for a lesser dream," because I could certainly identify the things I didn't want to settle for. I've seen too many people get hit with major obstacles or setbacks and then settle for much less than what their Greater Dreams had been. I didn't want that to happen in my life.

John seemed to need blunter and more sudden impacts to get his attention—like Lionel's passing and the incident with Colson's director. In contrast, most of my own forward movement came from gentle nudgings. When people have operated in my life the way my mother did—lovingly and gently, drawing the truth out of situations and then massaging it into me—I have found myself effectively learning spiritual truths and taking on new values.

Our pastor at the time of the crash, Del McKenzie, was someone who walked softly but inspirationally beside us. He inspired us to live the Greater Dream just with his presence. We were often great at coming up with good ideas, only perhaps to let them fall to the side when another one came along. Del would be the one to encourage us toward carrying the ideas to fruition and not letting them wither.

Del and his wife Jane always attended the barbecues, and each time they brought someone who was still exploring faith. That's the way Del operated. He supported us, and when he saw what we were actually up to with the barbecues, he got behind the idea and helped move it forward.

That became such an important part of not settling for the lesser dream. Just as I've seen people back away from their dreams because they tried it once and it blew up in their faces, I've seen others who have had great aspirations and great dreams, but in the middle of life coming at them from all sides the dreams have withered on the vine and died. Del believed in us, and that made all the difference.

Despite a good upbringing, I started out on very different footing from the security I have since found. If I had let the insecurity I felt early on dictate the script of my life, I would have settled for a lesser dream without ever knowing there was more that God wanted to accomplish with my one-and-only life. I'd have never tasted the beauty and richness of a life lived out of the depths of who God formed me to be.

If John had believed what that first evangelist told him, that he had nothing to offer except the ability to earn money and make donations, then he, too, would have settled for the lesser dream. But neither John nor I were willing to give up searching for that Greater Dream. The band U2 says it in their classic song: "I still haven't found what I'm looking for…"

Not too long ago, my brother Allen told us, "All my life I remember searching for something more, but I didn't know how to get there." At the time, John and I were together with him at an out-of-town retreat where we'd all been impacted. We were sitting together reflecting on some of the things we had just learned.

Allen told us how back in his Bible school days his desire to experience more of God had been so strong that he'd approached one of his teachers whom he thought was particularly spiritual and insightful.

"I told him how I felt, how I was looking for something more," Allen said to us, "and he just told me to go to bed. He said I'd feel better in the morning."

That did nothing to ease Allen's angst, of course.

"I knew my life had to count for something," he said. "I just didn't know how to get to that place."

He then told us about a time, years after the Bible school incident, when he was driving his tractor on the farm. He stopped the tractor in the middle of the field, overwhelmed again by this sense of there being "something more" that he just couldn't put his finger on. He got out of the cab, stood beside his tractor, and said, "Jesus, I've got to find somebody who can take me further. I want to go deeper, but I just don't know how to get there."

"Did God ever send that person?" I asked.

"Yes," Allen said, and he went on to mention the name of a leader in his community who has since become a close friend and mentor. Allen had pressed forward. Finally, he'd found someone who could help him explore the deeper things of his faith. The richness of their present relationship is a gift to Allen, and only God could have connected those pieces. Now he's experiencing a deeper and fuller relationship with Jesus and, therefore, a greater depth of living than he's ever known before.

The lesser experiences aren't wrong or bad; the problem comes when we settle for the lesser and give up on pursuing the "something more."

For instance, I spoke recently with a woman in her forties who was looking back at all the regrettable things she'd done in her life—affairs, wrong pursuits, and so on.

"Just think of all the time I've wasted!" she said to me.

She lamented the time that had slipped away, but quickly our conversation turned to the months and years still to come—the opportunities that lay ahead.

You see, the rest of the story is still unwritten. We know how we've lived our lives to this point, and we may even deeply regret some of the things we've done along the way. We're generally aware of what's happening in the present. The thing none of us can ever tell, though, is what will happen in the future, nor what our responses to that future will be—because our tomorrow is still unwritten until we actually engage it and live it out.

"Unwritten" means exactly that—the plot is not finalized, the characters are not all present, and the stage is not yet set.

Just prior to the crash, John and I were starting to get a taste of what living the Greater Dream was like. Hearing stories of people's life-changing experiences at the barbecues—that was satisfying and exciting. Watching couples' and families' newfound trust in God reshape their values and set them free from old ways which had bound them for years—that was immensely affirming and inspiring.

We would never have consciously chosen the crash to be the next chapter in our unwritten life story. But that's the thing about living life as human beings on planet Earth—stuff happens. When it does, what matters is how we respond to these unexpected and unwelcome circumstances. The way we walk forward is what determines the story that's written about us.

As I rode that cold Greyhound bus toward my family that winter day, tears streaming over my stitches, I have to admit that I was not at all thinking about my unwritten life. I was scared and feeling alone. If I thought anything at all about the Greater Dream, it was probably only that it was over. I just wanted us all to survive, and to be back with my husband so together we could figure out where to go from here. I was heading toward a New Normal that I neither understood nor wanted to explore.

The only faint glimmer of hope I could cling to was that I had seen us as a family touching the Greater Dream. I knew the dream was real; perhaps we could still get back to that place again. It was a very slim hope, and it was so fragile that I kept it tucked deep inside, almost afraid to admit it was even there. The decision to not settle for the lesser dream was foundational, and I knew we were going to need the strength of that foundation in the weeks and months ahead.

What I didn't know was how much.

Musings

CHAPTER 3

REALITY BITES

After arriving at the city hospital, I visited both my boys before going to see John, wanting to touch base with them and reconnect. But despite all the phone calls from the doctors during my week in the Whitecourt hospital, I was not prepared for what I found.

When I entered Brent's room, I could not believe what I saw. Although it was now sutured, the laceration on his shaved head stood out fiercely, running across the top of his skull. My little six-year-old, almost scalped! His leg was in traction, strung up by cords and pulleys, pointing forlornly at the ceiling. I stayed as long as I could, taking in the sight of my little boy, trying to adjust to this new reality. I finally had to tear myself away to go see my other son.

Compared to the hustle and bustle of Brent's ward, Byron's room was eerie in its relative silence. It took me several moments to come to grips with the fact that this still and silent form lying on the bed was actually my lively and fun-loving nine-year-old son.

A *click-tsssss* sound occurred over and over again. *Click-tsssssss*. Pause. *Click-tsssss*. The nurse had prepared me for what I'd find, but seeing my son in a coma, the respirator breathing for him, simply ripped into my heart. It was a deep and emotional pain, the extent of which I had never before experienced.

Repeatedly the respirator sounded, doing its work to keep the air moving in and out of Byron's little body. The sound became more than I could bear.

"Mrs. Baergen, why don't you come find a chair to rest in?"

A nurse had entered the room behind me and must have seen the despair, fear, and unutterable weariness I was feeling.

She smiled at me. "We could maybe even find a cot for you to have a sleep, if you'd like."

I shook my head. Hard as it was, I needed to be there for my son. He'd already been in this room close to a week with neither his father nor me by his side, and I hoped that maybe my presence would help awaken him. The original drug-induced coma, intended to let the doctors work on him more easily and let his healing process begin, had now given way to a natural coma, in which his little body was choosing to remain unresponsive to the world around him. I thought that if I stayed with him, somehow Byron would sense my presence and start to pull himself out of the coma. It was the only thing I could think of to do for my sweet little boy.

But nothing happened. I stayed for a long while, slow to let go of the hope that he would somehow miraculously respond to my being there.I had not grasped how devastating it would be for me to see my two boys in their hospital beds, and to realize their suffering. I felt as though I was betraying them as I left to find my husband.

As I trudged up the hallway toward the elevators, making my way to John's room, the feelings settling over me were beyond overwhelming. I felt—as a mother—that this was the worst thing I could ever have imagined. I thoroughly related to the biblical author Job and his statement, "That which I had greatly feared has come upon me."

And I hadn't even seen John yet.

* * * *

Lorraine stood beside my hospital bed, finally back with me after our seemingly endless time in two separate hospitals. I'd heard her come into the room, but my own facial injuries—smashed jaw and cheek bones, eyes still swollen pretty much shut—kept me from seeing her clearly. But hearing her voice confirmed that this was, indeed, Lorraine.

"Whatever happened, John?"

I could feel Lorraine searching for my hand with hers, and when she finally touched me I was overwhelmed with gratitude for the connection. At that moment it felt like somewhere a door had just closed and another had opened. At last the season of dealing with this myself—trying to make sense of it alone—was over. The realization that we'd begun what would become a life journey together was starting to settle in.

It was difficult to talk with my upper and lower jaws wired, but just having Lorraine there was comforting. I could feel emotional blockages deep inside slowly dissipating—things I hadn't even realized I was holding in. I started to feel like I could finally breathe deeply again.

After a long time of standing and just looking at me, Lorraine let go of my hand to slowly nudge a chair from the wall closer to the bed. I could tell by the way she gingerly sat down that her ribs were still bothering her; she winced a bit as she settled in.

"I had to come on the bus this morning because Jack's plane couldn't land yesterday," she said. "Carol came with me."

"I know," I said quietly through my wires, struggling for breath. "Jack told me."

"Oh, John!" Lorraine said. She felt again for my hand and took it in hers.

She stayed with me, occasionally speaking with air gathered painfully through broken ribs. I continued the battle to breathe, just holding on to life. Lorraine told me about seeing the boys before coming to my room; she tried to paint a clearer picture of how they were each doing, although she still struggled herself to understand. All I could register in my foggy, medicated brain, though, was that we were all alive.

Lorraine told me a bit about her time in Whitecourt, and about the intern stitching her face. It was still hard for me to understand what actually happened.

"I keep thinking this is a nightmare," Lorraine said at one point. "I wish I could just wake up and find everything back to normal."

I could feel the depth of her emotion even in my pharmaceutical daze. As raw as we both were emotionally, we drew strength from being together.

I recall when the doctor first gave us a glimpse into the future he thought was in store for us. He came into the room when Lorraine and I were together, took a deep breath, and in a professional yet caring way unpackaged his thoughts.

"I don't think John will ever walk again," he said. "If he does, it will be, at best, with two canes." He then described my injuries in more detail.

Lorraine told me later she could not comprehend the extent of change that lay ahead, so she simply chose to rest in the huge relief that I was alive and sharing this journey with her. It didn't really matter, anyway, what information we were hearing, or even what we were sharing back and forth. What was important, in that moment, was that we were together and reconnecting. Talking, staying quiet, just holding hands—all of it was our way of reaching out and finding each other again after being ripped apart so suddenly and devastatingly.

Being with Lorraine again, having her close, helped me understand a little more of what had happened to us. As the days went on, when my face wasn't as swollen and my eyes could focus again, I saw the extent of Lorraine's physical injuries. That helped me further come to terms with what we were walking through—or starting to walk through, anyway.

I still didn't fully realize, of course, how badly I was hurt. Pain was a constant companion, and the discomfort of lying in bed, not able to stretch my muscles, was growing stronger daily. I didn't yet know how badly my own face was crushed and battered.

Neither of us fully understood Byron's condition, despite the doctors trying to keep us informed. We were still at the stage of being thankful both boys were alive. The longer-term ramifications of what we'd have to face in the weeks and months ahead were unknown to us as we spent time quietly reconnecting in my hospital room. Deep down, I believe both of us expected a miracle. We were very familiar with stories of God's supernatural intervention in hopeless situations, and we fully believed our present experience would end with us becoming one of those miracle stories others told.

But as much as we were believing God for miraculous intervention, the harsh realities facing us demanded that we take practical steps. So, early in the recovery process, my friend Jack brought a lawyer into my hospital room. He offered legal counsel, knowing how difficult it would be for us to deal with the fallout from the car wreck. We trusted him immediately. He took our case on, to ensure that Byron's long-term needs would be addressed, and the long battle through the legal system began. It would be some time, however, before the results of this action played out.

Despite our inability to grasp the complexity that lay ahead, someone else knew well what life would be like for us as we rebuilt ourselves as individuals and as a family. Looking back, I strongly believe that God had already been at work for some time, preparing us to have the time and focus we'd need to begin the process of rebuilding our lives.

There were occasions in the year before the crash when it was very evident to me that God was up to something. It seemed God was directing his attention toward us and, more specifically, toward a foundational part of our lives—our character. He seemed to be redefining the spiritual DNA of our lives.

Farming was part of the Baergen tradition, and by the late 70s our farm had developed to where it was no longer a down-home family operation. I ran the farm strictly as one of my many businesses. The farm itself was large, and we kept it running at peak efficiency. My farm manager, Bill, was indispensable in those years because his skill in running the farm left me free to operate my other business pursuits.

Bill called me at the office one afternoon, saying he needed my help. Bill was a remarkably steady individual, so I wasn't accustomed to the tone of urgency and uneasiness I heard in his voice.

"The canola is all dry, ready to be harvested," he explained, "but the wind is starting to blow. A couple of my guys had a family emergency earlier in the day and I let them go home, but now we're really shorthanded and I'm concerned about this wind."

I could tell that Bill was really quite worried, and I understood why he would be. Canola is a field crop. When it's dry and ready for harvest, the stems and heads get very light and susceptible to wind. If a strong wind hits when the canola is ready, a whole field of grain can lift off the ground and roll up like a carpet, spinning like a giant tumbleweed right out of the field. And when it's gone, it's gone.

Our canola crop that year would be a significant source of farm revenue, and we had no insurance to cover this type of situation. This was a $100,000 crop, and most of it had been presold for seed. If it just up and blew away, our hope of recovering any of that income would blow away right with it.

"John, could you come and take over the combine for me?" Bill said. "We've got to get as much of this crop off as possible before the wind takes it."

With me to drive the combine, Bill and the other hand could keep both trucks going and just switch them when they were full. Without me, they'd have to shut down the operation waiting for the one truck to leave the field, empty its load, and return.

I dashed home, changed my clothes, and jumped into a half-ton truck to head out to the field. As I drew near, I could see that his assessment was accurate: the wind was really starting to blow, and the canola was lifting significantly.

I started praying.

I jumped out of the truck and dashed to the combine. As I ran up the ladder to the cab, Bill met me on his way down. I was praying fervently, asking God for help. I could see that without miraculous intervention, we were going to have a disaster on our hands.

But as soon as I shut the door to the cab, the wind started to die down. I could see the swaths of canola settle back, and in front of my eyes the situation reversed itself. I got back out of the cab and stood on the top step to see things from a different angle. It was true! The crop looked like it was going to be saved after all.

Bill slowly came back up the steps to the cab, looking at the same sight I was. He looked over at me.

"I know what *you* were doing!" he said with a big grin. I realized he meant the praying; I hadn't realized I was praying out loud.

Bill grinned again, slapped my back, and jumped back down the ladder to his truck. I got back into the cab, headed down the field, and the whole crop came off without further incident.

Bill was a good man. I trusted him implicitly, and he was strong, reliable, and the backbone of our farm operation. I knew God had been working on him for a while, moving him to consider spiritual matters. On that day, it was easy to see God at work in saving the canola crop, even for Bill, but as I sat in the cab that afternoon and guided the slow-moving machine up and down the field, I had a lot of time to think. God was up to something, but I couldn't see yet what He had in mind. I knew, though, that He was concerned with making a difference in more than just the canola.

While I could see God was speaking into Bill's life, loving him and wanting him to know how much he was loved, there was no way I could see God also grooming Bill's commitment to me and to us as a family. God really knew what He was doing in laying a foundation for us that whole year. He knew what was coming and was helping us prepare for it, as much as we would let Him.

In the months after the crash, as I started to realize the ways God had built a strong foundation for us ahead of time, I wondered why He had done it that way. Why intervene in ways that would prepare us for something, only to let the catastrophe occur? Couldn't He just as easily have stepped in and stopped the tragedy from unfolding?

God used another incident to further cement things with Bill. He was an excellent manager, as I've said, and we considered him and his amazing wife

Karen to be friends. I knew I could trust him to keep things at the farm in top condition. At the same time, the farm was home for me, and often in the evenings or on the weekend, after a hectic week in the business world, I'd change into my grubbies and help out wherever I was needed, just to unwind.

I came into the lower yard one day and found the remains of a clean-up fire smouldering. The weather was still fairly warm, and with the air as hot and dry as it had been that week, I thought the fire had been set too close to one of the grain bins. I noticed Bill coming out of one of the equipment sheds in the lower yard.

"Hey, Bill," I said. "You've been doing a bit of clean-up?"

"Yes," he said. "Ever since we talked about expanding the grain handling system, I've been working to give the trucks better access to the bins. I cleared the areas around these bins today, and burning it all seemed the best way to get rid of the overgrowth I pulled out."

I eyed the smouldering pile. "Do me a favour, would you?" I asked. "I think you should kill this fire. It's still smouldering, and I think it's a bit close to the bins."

Bill looked at the pile of burned stumps for a bit before he turned to me again. "Hey, John," he said, "no offence, but you run your office—I'll run the farm."

I left it at that, because, he was right. He knew what he was doing, and the farm was running at least as well if not better than it had been before I brought Bill on board. I never had to worry when Bill was running things.

A couple of days later, I returned home after being out of town on a business trip. I was pulling into the house yard when Lorraine stepped out of the house to meet me.

"Now, John, stay calm," she said to me as I got out of the car.

"Why? What's up?"

"Well, the lower yard was burned out today. A fire got away on Bill."

The lower yard housed several grain bins, the barn, and a storage granary. I handed my briefcase to Lorraine, got back in the car, and drove down to the site.

Almost everything was destroyed. From what I could see, the only thing untouched was the big barn. Where yesterday we'd had full bins of grain, now we were left with blackened building frames, smoking heaps of ruined canola, and black and white piles of rubble and ash. The heaps of rubble still smouldered, despite the huge puddles of water that showed someone had fought hard to save things.

"I guess I'm fired, eh?"

I turned around. Bill and Karen's house was near the lower yard, and Bill had come out when he heard me pull up, wiping his black hands on a rag. Soot still streaked his face and clothing. I turned back to survey the damage again.

"No, no, Bill, you're not fired." I surveyed the rubble, trying to estimate a cost for what we'd lost. Then I looked Bill right in the eye. "But I sure hope you learned from this!"

Bill told me later—a lot later—that the whole fire experience and how I'd reacted was a defining moment for him. That experience, combined with the answer to prayer he'd seen with the canola, prompted him to become an intentional follower of Jesus not long after.

When our lives changed so drastically the following year, our trust in Bill and Karen—and their commitment to us—had been ingrained deeply. Bill's ability to keep our central farm operation running while we were rebuilding our lives became key to our survival. It was definitely part of the preparation God was building into us for what was to come.

To this day, I think of Bill as my kid brother.

Reflecting on how God prepared and refined us ahead of time, I've seen repeatedly that He knows what He is doing—and that He really can be trusted. While I'm limited to seeing only the here and now, He can see the end of the journey from the beginning. He knows the potential of everything coming in the unwritten future, and He knows how strong a foundation we'll need in order to face it. It's been a slow process for me, but I'm finally able to relax in the knowledge that He cares deeply about me. The more I'm able to embrace that truth today, the better foundation I have for writing the unwritten portion of my story tomorrow.

*　　*　　*　　*

I've often found myself walking a different journey from John, even when we're going in the same direction, side by side on the same road.

I know for certain that God was involved in preparing us in the months leading up to the car wreck, but the things I became most aware of were centred around our family. In fact, God wasn't just preparing me for what Byron was going to walk through; He was preparing Byron himself. I love that He cares for us each in the way that is best for us individually.

I marvel at the masterful way God weaves seemingly insignificant threads together to create a tapestry of love and compassion. Like a handmade quilt, God's tapestry can be put in a special place—admired but not needed—until the power goes off on a cold winter night. Then the quilt brings comfort and warmth to anyone touched by it.

I'd been checked out of the Whitecourt hospital after only one week in care. Likely it was too early a release for the state I was in, with my face still in stitches and my ribs broken, but I'm sure the medical staff in Whitecourt decided I'd be better off with my family.

The cold reality was certainly sinking in now. I was shocked at the extent of John's injuries. Always a strong man, he seemed just a broken shell, almost unrecognisable due to his extensive facial injuries. After that initial dose of reality, I quickly shifted my thinking to figuring out how we were going to move forward. John's appearance no longer really registered with me. It definitely hurt me to see his pain, but then I'd feel overwhelming relief that he was alive, and that he could continue to share this journey with me.

Our pastor was a key support for us throughout our time in hospital, especially in the early weeks. His were a set of footsteps John came to recognize, the distinct sound of Del McKenzie's cowboy boots echoing through the hallway long before he actually entered the room. It was a long trip from our hometown to the city hospital, but Del would make it regularly. In the early days, he'd sit by John's bed in silence, just letting his presence comfort us. That silence truly was a healing comfort for us. Sometimes, even now, we'll find ourselves visiting someone in hospital or grieving a loss, and when we feel uncomfortable, not knowing what to say, we'll recall Del's quiet presence all those years ago. We'll remember again that sometimes just being there, not saying anything, can be the greatest encouragement.

Del knows the Bible inside and out, and every once in a while during a visit he'd quietly start to quote from it—not reading, just speaking it word for word and line by line. That was more strengthening than I can describe. I don't think it would have been as powerful if he'd been reading from the written page—somehow the recitation from memory brought a comfort to it we'd never known before.

Other people's reactions to John's appearance, however, were sometimes so overwhelming they were almost comical. Just before I arrived in Edmonton, John was visited by our lawyer and a banker buddy of his who were on their way home from a fun little jaunt down to Vegas. Our lawyer friend had heard about our wreck, and thought he'd take advantage of travelling through the city by stopping in to visit John at the hospital.

John told me the story later. He'd heard the footsteps approaching his bed, and was pleased to hear our friend's voice as the two men got closer to the room. Visitors to that point had been mainly family.

Both men approached John's bed; their eyes widened abruptly as they saw him, and almost like choreography they both turned and bolted from the room. John said he could hear double sets of running footsteps echoing back from the hallway, followed by the sound of a door opening and closing.

Our lawyer and his friend didn't come back that day. In fact, it wasn't until several weeks later that he sheepishly shared his story. Apparently, both he and his buddy were feeling slightly off-kilter to begin with, having just returned from what sounded like a very boisterous time in Las Vegas. When they got close enough to John's bed to see his face clearly, they were both overcome by what they saw. Their mad dash down the hallway was to find a bathroom, and they'd literally battled each other at the doorway to see who could get in first. If anyone had followed them down the hallway, our friend said, they would have found both of them retching wildly.

It was probably better we hadn't known their reaction at the time.

Despite his broken appearance, I could see John was still the same strong man inside. His determination to pull through and live was more evident every day. Even though I had fewer physical injuries, I was literally overwhelmed in those early days after the crash. As I made my way back and forth from John's room to Byron's room, with brief side trips to Brent's room, I could feel the full force of our tragedy pressing in on me.

But God had already taken care of yet another detail. My sister Carol and I had both studied nursing, and a great deal of our studies had taken place in these very hallways at the Royal Alexandra Hospital, or the "Royal Alex" as we called it. As my trips around the facility became routine, I began bumping into nurses I'd trained with. It was a little thing, compared to all that had happened, but having some friends at the hospital really gave me a lift. My former nursing instructor, still on this ward, also helped me better understand the medical realities we faced. My emotional freefall seemed to slow slightly.

But it was the preparation God had undertaken with Byron that really stood out to me when I reflected back months and years later. Seemingly random and insignificant events became solid handholds and footholds we could cling to when we finally started to get our bearings and climb out of the canyon of crisis.

Byron and Brent were wonderful boys. I'm sure every mother would say the same about her children, but I honestly saw a unique bond between the two of them. Byron was three years older than Brent, and the age difference was enough to let Brent see his big brother as a true hero—but it was not a big enough difference to keep them from playing together, which they did regularly and with abandon.

At nine years of age, Byron was already starting to transition from little-boy-only thinking to the deeper thought processes that mark a more mature soul.

I remember having one conversation with Byron when he came to me wondering what the Holy Spirit did. It wasn't like we'd been spending time as a family discussing these things, but somewhere Byron had picked up on it. He'd always had a sensitive spirit.

I did my best to explain it in a way a nine-year-old could understand.

"Well, Byron," I said, "the Holy Spirit is God, just like God the Father and Jesus are God."

I could see him trying to think that one through.

"Cool!" he said.

I continued, explaining that when the Holy Spirit takes control, He gives us power to live our Christian lives.

Byron liked that. "Boy, Mom, that's what I need!"

He was excited to ask the Holy Spirit to take control of his life and to give him power to live as Jesus directed him. I told him we needed to wait until his dad got home so we could all pray together. I didn't know how much six-year-old Brent had taken in or understood while he'd listened in on the end of our conversation, but for weeks after he talked about the "three Jesuses."

Sure enough, when John came home Byron was eager to have us all pray, so we spent time as a family asking the Holy Spirit to give Byron power in his life.

The next day, as was our routine, I drove to the rural bus stop to pick the boys up after school. When the bus door opened, Byron literally jumped out, ran full tilt to where I was parked, and slid to a stop.

"Hey, guess what, Mom?" he said excitedly. "Today Derrick asked Jesus into his life!"

Byron told me that he and his buddy Derrick had been in the school washroom together when they heard a radio report claiming the world would end that day at 6:05 p.m. (To this day, I still don't know what that was about!) Byron's buddy had asked Byron what he should do, and Byron responded, "Ask Jesus into your life!"—which he did, with Byron's help.

"Mom," he said, "without the Holy Spirit's power I could never have done that!"

Byron was amazed by the whole experience, and marked in a profound way.

There was another incident that confirmed for me how God had been preparing us, establishing our trust for future challenges.

One Monday morning, Byron accompanied me on a trip to town while I deposited the month's cheques at three different banks—one batch for the farm, another for the other businesses, and the third for our personal accounts. It was an early spring day, warming up but still grey and blustery, and the wind was at gale force as we made our rounds.

I was at the teller's counter at the first bank when I realized some of the cheques for that particular deposit were missing. I figured they'd been mixed in with the rest of the papers in the car, so I sent Byron out to get the whole pile. He brought all the papers in, I found the cheques, and everything else went smoothly.

The second bank transaction went without a hitch, and we headed off to do the third.

At the third bank, where we did our personal banking, I discovered another cheque was missing. According to my deposit slip, it was a cheque for nearly $2,000, and I knew we needed that money in the bank to cover a cheque I'd written at church the day before. I also knew John had already endorsed the cheque, so whoever came across it could cash it.

Needless to say, I was more than a little concerned! There were no other papers in the car now, because this was our last stop, so I knew the cheque had vanished somewhere during our morning travels.

My first thought was that Byron must have dropped it back at the first bank when he brought the pile of papers in—and my reaction was not one I'm proud of.

"Byron, what did you do with that cheque?" I said to my son. It had been at least half an hour since we had been at the first bank, but all I could think to do was to retrace our steps and see if we could find anything. We needed to have that money in our account that day! We drove back to the first bank and parked near where we had been earlier.

As we got out of the car, Byron noticed a little whirlwind—one of those mini twisters—swirling near his car door. He stepped out, reached his hand into the spinning dust and litter, and grabbed a piece of paper that had been blowing around and around.

"What's this, Mom?" he said, holding the paper out to me.

It was the cheque.

I believe that experience was part of God's plan to prepare Byron for the tough journey that lay just around the corner. It was a situation God had allowed Byron and us to participate in so we would trust Him in far more challenging circumstances. God had reminded us that nothing is hopeless when He's part of the equation, and that He does hear us when we pray. The trust Byron learned that day has held him strong through the years.

I treasured that experience, and thought about it many times in the years that lay ahead of us.

Just a week before the crash, God was still preparing us.

Christmas dinner was always a big deal in the Baergen household, and that year was no different. We put a high value on family time, especially at Christmas, but our table at dinner was always open to others from within each of our spheres of influence.

Although I'd grown up in a very safe and stable family, I was incredibly shy in my early years as a wife and mother. I often felt insecure and threatened by the fast-paced world in which I lived. But not John! He was always striking up new friendships and relationships. It soon became customary for us to function as an extended family on special occasions. If a major holiday was near at hand, we would regularly toss out invitations for people to come join us at our dinner table. Most of the people would show up, too! The doorbell would ring, some stranger would say, "Hi, is this the Baergen house? We're so and so!"— and another guest or two would join us. Although it would not have been my first lifestyle choice, I have to admit I grew to love having extra people around. They filled our house with joy and laughter.

I remember my sisters Carol and Terri being with us that year, along with a fellow who worked as a driller on the Alberta oil rigs. One of the local radio stations had hired a new deejay, who'd just arrived in town before the holidays, and Carol had befriended him and invited him over as well.

The newest rage on the techno-toys market that year was a particular electronic game, and Byron had received one for Christmas. He really enjoyed it, and after dinner he'd cornered the deejay and showed him how it worked and how to play the various games.

From the kitchen where I was cleaning up, I could hear their conversation. They were chatting about the game when Byron suddenly took things in a different direction.

"Do you know much about Jesus?" Byron asked.

"Uhh, not really," the deejay said.

"How come?"

"Well, I've never really thought about it before."

As I listened, my nine-year-old son launched into a discussion about faith with this young radio personality.

Like Jesus' mother Mary in the Bible, I treasured and pondered these things in my heart. In the midst of the actual events, of course—the Holy Spirit questions, the experience with the cheque, the conversations about faith between my nine-year-old and a deejay in his late twenties—I saw them only as isolated occurrences, profound and wonderful, but merely evidence of my son's growing maturity. Later, I was able to discern how God had been at work building a foundation of trust in both my heart and Byron's for the hard months and years that were to come.

Despite our inability to recognize what was happening, God, my Heavenly Father, knew the heartache that was about to descend upon us. He knew the depths of despair we would sink into before things started to ease. He knew, too, the extreme physical and emotional challenges we were going to experience, and in numerous ways He strengthened our foundation without us even being aware of it.

God chose to honour the freewill He gave us as human beings. He did not step in when a drunken man decided to get behind the wheel of his truck and head out on the highway that tragic New Year's Day. But at the same time, our Heavenly Father also chose to take the time He needed to build into each of us the foundation we would need for our journey. I now see that as His love and deep care in action for us; but, yes, it took me a long time to see that for what it was.

I didn't cry when I visited the hospital that first week. But almost every night, when I was alone in my room away from the hospital, I wept uncontrollably. I just couldn't comprehend what was happening—and why. I ached for it all to be over.

Through it all, God was still at work in me. Despite being deeply wounded, in my tenderness I felt very close to God—closer, in fact, than I had ever felt before. I longed to become all He had planned for me to be. In spite of all that had happened, that longing stayed in me—quietly, yes, but deeper and stronger than the pain I was working through.

Musings

CHAPTER 4

DREAMS DIE

"**W**hat the !@#$%^& is going on here?"

Every eye in the room snapped to Dr. Arthur Cagney's face as he strode across the room toward my bed. As an orthopaedic surgeon, he commanded respect to begin with—but his current level of anger caused everyone to stiffen as they waited to see what he would do next.

It had already been a harrowing morning. It was my second week in the hospital, and a shift in priorities was in the works regarding my medical care. From the beginning, the real concern had been my very survival. Now it appeared I might actually live, so the trauma/survival teams were gradually giving over care to the longer-term rehabilitation team.

Priority One: make sure the patient will be able to walk again.

The decision was made to pin my leg and put me in traction, realigning my pelvis and legs to a more normal position as they healed. X-rays were examined, the surgeon determined the position for the pin to be inserted, the anaesthetist froze the site, and the intern went to work with a drill.

But through an extreme case of miscommunication or error, the place where the freezing had been injected and the place where the drill bit chewed into my leg were two different spots. The pain was excruciating! The smell was unbearable, too, and by the time the pin was put into place I'd gone into shock.

Dr. Cagney came as soon as the error was discovered. I was pretty much out of it at that point, but I could still hear what was going on in the room. "You stupid @#$%!" he yelled. "Look at the indications on the leg where the freezing is, and then look where you drilled..." He continued cussing rather profoundly.

When I became fully aware again, Dr. Cagney explained to Lorraine and me what had happened, and outlined the recovery plan from that point forward.

The one positive thing from this situation was that Dr. Cagney took on the direct oversight of my case. Every day I became part of his rounds, and when everything was finally done it was he who came and took my leg out of traction.

This was a rude jolt of transition into the post-survival world. Through that whole first week, I'd been fully aware of being held in the arms of Jesus; I had a clear sense of comfort and peace. But now I was moving into reality—a new reality. And, quite frankly, this reality sucked.

I was not the first or only person to experience the harshness of life in the real world. At the time, however, I didn't have the luxury of sitting in an easy chair with a nice cup of coffee, pondering the ins and outs of what was happening in our lives. The pain was constant, the day-to-day progress was incremental and sometimes unnoticeable, and the silence from heaven was deafening. What in the world was happening? And why was God allowing it?

I still felt that sense of being held, but God certainly wasn't responding to my pleas for understanding or explanation. The fog of those early days was lifting, yet the picture I was left with was anything but clear: God wasn't swooping in to fix everything so I could learn my lesson and carry on with life.

Ever since my non-meeting with Chuck Colson, I had been growing in my faith, my spiritual awareness, and my prayer life. The routine I'd unconsciously established was pretty cut and dry: I lived and worked to the max, confident that God would respond to my prayers about either problems or opportunities—because I'd seen Him do it over and over.

Yet now I was faced with the greatest obstacles I'd ever known, and God was remaining noticeably silent through the whole ordeal—glaringly and obviously silent. My whole family was in severe pain, physically and emotionally, and God was not rushing in to deal with the torment and make things right.

As the fog lifted, I spent more and more time trying to dialogue with God, trying to engage with the One I knew had the answers to my urgent questions.

But I was getting nothing.

It was like being in a greenhouse. I could sense His warmth and care, yet there seemed to be a glass wall preventing my prayers from getting through.

In the strangest way, I began to experience real desolation. I was living in a dichotomy like never before; I was still sensing the arms of Jesus holding me, yet facing agonizing loneliness as I watched life spiral out of control around me. It wasn't as though God was giving me answers I didn't want to hear—He wasn't acknowledging me at all. And although I was only vaguely aware of it in those first couple of weeks, even my business pursuits were stumbling, suffering in the onset of the growing recession and not having the attention of either Lorraine or me to keep things on track. God wasn't doing anything about that, either.

In what felt like adding insult to injury, both my cheekbones became infected, and huge amounts of antibiotics were needed to keep the infection under control. I continued to push harder and deeper for some response from God, some sense that He knew what was happening and was preparing to step in. But there was nothing.

The silence became, if anything, even louder.

Looking back, I can see that God truly was at work, but certainly not in the ways I was used to. If I were to use athletic terms to describe my spiritual progress before the crash, I would say that I'd always been a sprinter. I was used to being on the track with a short, clearly defined distance to run, accustomed to putting everything I had into the crucial drive to the finish, ready to dig deep, push hard, and blaze through to victory.

Now God was asking something new of me, something that required different spiritual muscles and a new game plan. A sprinter has a different body type than a marathon runner: the muscles used in the drive to cross that 100-metre mark contrast noticeably with those needed to endure the agonizing miles of a long-distance run. I'm reminded of that every time I watch the Olympics and see the lanky and lean marathoners enter the stadium for the final leg of their incredible journey, circling around on the same track where, on another day, the big-muscled sprinters blazed their way to the finish line.

The races themselves are worlds apart, too. A sprinter hears the roar of the crowd for the full length of the contest, and the results of the race are clear within ten seconds of the starter's pistol shot. A marathoner, on the other hand, may hear the occasional cheer of encouragement from the sidelines, but the full support of the crowd isn't felt until the final moments of the event, which comes long hours after the initial surge out of the gate. While there are certainly other competitors to deal with in any race, a marathon runner's biggest challenger is often the one he carries with him on the inside—the one whose voice pounds in his ears mile after mile when no one else is around.

Having lived life as a sprinter, I wasn't prepared for the agony of building the muscles needed for my marathon. Nor was I prepared to have a coach who wouldn't let me know the destination ahead of time or tell me how to get there, who was silent even while He worked on me.

And He *was* at work, even when all I could hear was silence. I know that now, of course, but back in the hospital, my marathon training was just getting underway. The first part of the workout routine had me learning how to persevere even when I couldn't understand what the coach was doing or hear His answers to my desperate questions.

I didn't realize there were regions even deeper than "desperate." To this day, I can't even put a name to some of those deeper regions, but I know it was in those moments that I started to make my choice to walk forward in faith, even when I was hearing nothing. My "sprinter faith"—happy with the roaring crowd and the rush of victory after the drive to the finish—was giving way to "marathon faith." I was learning what it meant to take one more step forward, mile after mile, even when everything inside was screaming to stop because of the pain.

Around this time, something started to percolate in me, something even deeper than faith. As the days passed, faith continued to be strong in me. I knew God was still present, even though I wasn't hearing Him respond to our situation in any noticeable ways. I still had genuine assurance that I belonged to Him. Everything beyond that, however, was simply a walk of faith—and I had to keep moving forward, even though I had no certainty there'd be anything under my feet in the next step. The silence continued, and it was ominous.

In those long days and nights of being confined to bed, while the doctors poked, prodded, and pulled to help my body heal properly, I had a lot of time to muse over our predicament. God had gone silent, from my perspective, yet I stood firmly on my faith. Like a momentary clearing of the haze, every once in a while the awareness that there was something at work in me even deeper than solid faith would catch me by surprise. Then, seconds later, the clear view, and the insight it brought, would disappear into the next bank of fog.

Had I been asked about it, I wouldn't have been able to explain these glimmers beyond saying that I felt like a child starting to realize the world was bigger than he thought it was. I couldn't say how, but my comprehension of living a life of faith was changing even without my full awareness.

Why couldn't God have sent me a letter, or highlighted a specific paragraph from the Bible that would have given me all the answers I needed? Even a dream from Him, detailing in visual yet cryptic ways an understanding of what we were going through, would have been welcome. But no, He'd shifted to being my marathon coach, and even though I sometimes wanted to shout at Him in frustration, He continued to remain silent. He simply stayed with me as I went through the agonizing periods and events necessary to my healing.

Restless by nature, I was glad when I could finally escape the hospital for an occasional breather. Once spring set in, it was easier for me to venture outside, although I was so messed up physically that I tried to stay out of sight as much as possible!

I loved taking every opportunity to step out. I'd get a pass from the nursing station and totter out of the hospital on crutches, barely able to keep my balance, but elated that I was tasting freedom. Near the hospital was the old MacDonald Hotel, to which Lorraine sometimes took me for a change of scenery and menu—although with my mouth wired shut I couldn't eat solid food. I recall one time being on an escalator while I was still on crutches, teetering on the edge of losing my balance, but giddy over the fact that I was away from the hospital. Other times I would be taken to McDonald's, either just with Lorraine or with family and friends joining us, and I would hide behind a tree and enjoy the taste of a "real" milkshake.

Eventually the time came to take the wires out of my face and jaw. Because of the severe impact it had received, my face had changed from what it was like before the crash. Doctors had wired my upper and lower jaws together to stabilize my face in an appropriate position to allow mending to occur.

"You'll need to be prepared for this, John," said the doctor. "There will be a lot of blood flow as we pull the wires out, and we won't be able to give you any anaesthetic. You'll need to be as alert as possible so you don't choke on the blood."

I understood his words, but I couldn't fully comprehend the ramifications of what he was telling me.

"John, I need you to understand: this will be extremely painful, and we cannot give you anything for the pain." The surgeon was standing at the foot of my bed, looking intently into my eyes.

Man alive. I appreciated his concern, but I thought he was perhaps being melodramatic. Didn't he know how much pain I'd already been through? Surely there was nothing I hadn't already experienced in the pain department. Just having the wires in my jaw had been painful. Various infections had cropped up around the wire entry points, and sometimes my head had been so swollen it almost looked like a balloon!

Although I was really looking forward to having the wires out, I was starting to get the point that the removal process wasn't going to be very pleasant.

I remembered our pastor years before telling his story. He, too, had had wires removed from his face, and he told of excruciating pain and blood loss. In that process, he'd remembered the story of Jesus as He moved into the final hours before His death on the cross. As I lay there, my mind also settled on that account.

In the hours before He died, Jesus knew what was going to happen and He agonized over it to the point where His sweat was like drops of blood. I realized any pain I was about to go through would pale in comparison to His experience.

And so we did it.

Lorraine sat anxiously in the waiting room during the procedure. I should have known how intense it was going to be when the doctor said he didn't want Lorraine to be present.

Two nurses came to hold my hands, one on each side, and the doctor and his team went to work snipping the wires and pulling them out.

The goriness was unbelievable. The pain was unimaginable. The amount of blood was something I had never seen before in my life—and this was my own blood. It didn't take long for me to go into shock from the unfathomable pain. The last thing I remember thinking in my agony was, *Jesus, I can't even grasp what you went through! And you chose to do it for me!*

It took ages for me to be able to even talk about what I went through, even with Lorraine. Experiences like that went too deep; some things you cannot talk about for the longest time.

This marked the start of numerous surgeries and unending therapy for me—procedures that continue even now. Certainly the length of time between surgeries has increased over the years, but these realities stay with me as part of my daily journey. The trials my family and I have gone through, and the lessons we've come to grips with, are never far from the surface, and they're brought home to me afresh every time I walk through the doors of a hospital for yet another corrective procedure.

It seemed like we always had a lot of people visiting us. Early on, a doctor named Jim Mabbot heard about our family through the medical grapevine. Though he wasn't one of our physicians, he took it upon himself to pop in and visit whenever he was nearby. He was a wonderful support, quiet and strong, and it always did my heart good to hear his footsteps approaching my door.

Lorraine divided her time between my room and the boys' rooms, and other visitors tended to congregate around me. The number of people visiting, or the length of their stays, sometimes became too much for me, so I devised a plan with the nurses on my ward. If I was finding the company overwhelming, I'd catch the eye of one of the nurses and give a quick wink. That meant, "Please get these people out of here!"

With my graduation out of traction and into a wheelchair, I was finally able to go see Byron, who'd been in a coma since the crash. It took a bit of planning, but one day I evaded the visitors in my own room and set off to see my son. Jim Mabbot, the physician, came into the hospital early that day and met me at the front desk. He stayed with me the whole time, just to be a support while I visited Byron.

That day, the penny dropped for me. When I wheeled into Byron's room and saw the high-powered son I remembered simply lying there forlornly, I lost it. I remember Jim being beside my chair, but more vividly I recall the intense emotions coursing through me at seeing my son lying so absolutely still on his bed.

I wept and wept at the sight. We'd been handling this recovery journey for close to six weeks now, but for the first time I realized the full extent of Byron's injuries and, correspondingly, the severity of our situation. It was quite a watershed moment for me.

Deeply despondent, I wheeled slowly back to my room. Jim had stayed with me the whole time, not saying a word. His emotional support was more important than any words he could have spoken.

I bottomed out for a couple days after that. The change in Byron was devastating—once a vibrant nine-year-old, now a still and virtually lifeless form lying on a hospital bed. The respirator that kept him breathing was gone, but also gone was his awareness of everything and everyone around him. My little boy was totally closed off from me.

For a while after seeing Byron, it was hard for me to focus, but for the most part my own healing was progressing well.

* * * *

My heart, too, was full of sadness for our dear Byron, although in a more noticeable way than John was experiencing, and definitely closer to the surface. I had basically moved to the city after being discharged from the Whitecourt hospital. Day after day I'd be in Byron's room, hoping against hope that he was aware of my presence, but receiving no indication that he was.

My emotions were all over the place. Gratitude for our survival coursed through me at one moment, only to be replaced in the next by horror at the situation or frustration at the slowness of recovery. I'd experience love, and even the occasional laugh, as John and Brent recovered to the point where we could actually reengage as a family; I'd carry these positive emotions to Byron's bedside, wanting desperately for him to sense and respond to the love I brought with me. Then the hours would go by, with the deadening sameness of his current existence settling over me, and once again any small resource of hope I'd brought with me would dissipate into nothingness. Yet, those hours of stillness gave me opportunity to look deeply inside myself and see internal strength begin to take root.

Being one of six kids growing up, I knew what it was like to be part of a high-energy family that played together and worked together. Unlike John, though, I hadn't developed a personality that made me want to stand out in a crowd and climb to the top; I was happy to inhabit the background, more comfortable not being the centre of attention.

My home was very Jesus-centred, and each and every week included at least one church service—usually more. Dad was really plugged in at the church, always leading in one capacity or another, and rarely was there a church event my dad didn't attend. I think he would have been happiest if we'd all gone with him to everything, but that wasn't always possible for a young and growing family. Even so, we showed up at most church meetings.

I have to admit, it got to the point where I resented church, because it engaged my dad's full attention. Still, our family's heavy involvement in a faith community did contribute to the stable home in which I enjoyed growing up.

And our home was secure. I remember that feeling well.

I remember my dad's faithfulness. When I think back to the earliest memories I have of him, apart from his strong commitment to the church, I always picture the times when I'd wake up early in the morning only to find he'd already been up for a long time before me, Bible open, just starting his day in spiritual contemplation.

Some of my earliest recollections of my mother are the times she'd tell us stories as the six of us kids sat around the kitchen table. Sometimes she'd read to us out of her well-worn Bible, pausing to interject explanations or details that made the stories come alive. Other times, she told simple tales of life and wonder—but all the time, in every story she told, everything had to do with values. Some of my ways of thinking, to this very day, stem from those times around the kitchen table where I learned the wisdom of life and faith from my mother's stories.

My own journey with Jesus started after one of those story times with my mom, back when I was just six years old. After reading to us, Mom tucked us into bed and left to check on something elsewhere in the house.

My brother heard me crying and asked what was wrong. Several of my other siblings also heard, and called for my mom to come back into the room.

"I want to ask Jesus into my life," I sobbed, feeling the immensity of God's love for me and wanting someday to be with Jesus in heaven.

My mother understood what was happening, and knelt at my bedside to lead me in a prayer of giving my life to Jesus. Even though I was young, I knew right away that my life would be marked by this experience.

That was a Saturday night. The next day, Sunday, was a regular church day, although for me it was anything but regular! I sat in the middle of the car's back seat the whole way to church, wiggling and squirming with anticipation. As soon as we got to the church parking lot, I scrambled over whichever sister was beside me and jumped out the door to run to tell my friends the exciting news.

Jesus had made a significant impact on me, and I told everyone I could see that I'd asked Him into my life. To this day, my closest childhood friend tells me it was that morning, seeing me so full of joy and childlike expectation, that significantly influenced her to make the same decision.

All in all, our home life was solid. I felt secure in my family, secure in my parents' commitment to love Jesus.

Despite this sense of stability, however, I wasn't very secure or confident in who I was developing into. Somehow, even with this new reality of Jesus in my life, I found myself growing up to become a shy, insecure woman filled with many unsubstantiated fears.

I struggled a lot as I grew older. I'd often give in to the opinions of others, even if they differed from my own; then I'd be critical of myself for doing so. I wasn't always a pushover, because I did share ideas and opinions when I felt safe—but only when I felt safe. Most often, I'd just keep those thoughts to myself.

I recall one nursing instructor, frustrated that I never participated in class discussion, putting it this way: "You are selfish. You listen to every other person's thoughts, yet you never speak your own." Interestingly, as a nursing student, despite my outward insecurities, deep inside I felt great empathy for the patients I cared for, and was often able to lead them toward a better frame of mind in their recovery process. To my surprise, I was given the award for outstanding performance in psychiatric nursing at my graduation ceremony.

When I analyze what I thought and felt back then, I'd say that more than anything I lived in fear—although I couldn't have articulated that at the time. I was afraid of what other people might think. I was afraid of saying the wrong thing, or doing the wrong thing, or, in fact, of letting people down in any way. I was afraid of becoming the centre of attention. I was afraid of being left out. I was afraid of making decisions that might later turn out to be wrong. Fear influenced every choice I made.

And fear, I know now, is the opposite of faith. I knew Jesus was an integral part of my life, and I lived out my faith in virtually all the things we were involved with. Yet most of my thoughts reflected my fearfulness of knowing the right thing to say or do, or whether I'd be able to face any difficulty that came at us.

Now my very worst fears had been realized: my precious boys, my adorable little six- and nine-year-old sons, were seriously injured and lying in a hospital. My pillar of strength, the man upon whom I'd always known I could depend for the courage to walk me through just such a catastrophe as this, was also lying broken and on the edge of the grave. I felt I'd been left alone to deal with the massive ramifications of what had just happened to us as a family.

I wasn't really alone, of course. My dear family, John's family, our close friends, and our extended church family were there in every way they could be, eager to stand with us and walk with us along this unfamiliar road.

Yet, in a deeper and more profound way, I really was alone—alone with no one to truly depend upon. Alone, that is, except for God, who was now able to step over the fears and broken support systems I had built for myself through the years and move into my life more deeply and fully than I could ever have envisioned before. He had been there for me all along of course, desiring to come alongside and shape me spiritually into the woman He had designed me to be and had always known I could be. But in my shy, insecure, fearful way, I'd resisted Him. Now, with my life literally shattered to pieces around me, His spiritual shaping could at last proceed in earnest.

*   *   *   *

A rehabilitation hospital, the Glenrose, was attached to the Royal Alex by an underground passageway. After about three weeks in general treatment, I was transferred there to start mobility therapy. Early on, Lorraine had been told I'd never walk again, so my time at the Glenrose was particularly important to me. I was determined to prove the doctors wrong.

I poured what little energy I had into rehabilitation, determined to master each new round of physio exercises. That defined my life in that period—physio from morning to night, only to wake the next morning and begin the routine all over again.

Soon after I arrived at the Glenrose, a man named Jerry was brought in and given the bed next to mine. Jerry was about forty-five, a tough-looking oil man. Having lost one leg earlier, he was having his second leg amputated due to a blood disorder. We got to know each other well, as my ability to talk had improved significantly by then.

On the first or second night Jerry was there, after the nurses organized him for the night and the ward was growing quiet, I heard him crying softly. I leaned forward to where I could reach the curtain between our beds, and pulled it back so I could talk with him.

"Hey, buddy," I said. "Are you okay?"

"No, I'm not," Jerry said. "I drove here to the hospital by myself because I've got no one else. My wife told me she can no longer handle all the challenges in our lives, so she's leaving me. I'm not doing very good."

For a moment, I became my pre-crash bold self. "Jerry, the only answer is Jesus—there is nothing else."

We chatted a little more, and then Jerry became quiet.

"Okay, Baergen, how do I do this Jesus thing?"

"You just give your life to Him," I said. Jerry looked at me blankly. I tried again. "Jerry, just tell God you want to take yourself out of the driver's seat of your life, so to speak, and turn control over to Him."

"Can you do that with me?" he asked. I reached across the bed, we joined hands, and I led him in a simple prayer, during which he turned his life over to Jesus.

The next morning, Jerry's bed was empty, and when he returned later in the afternoon his second leg was gone.

I was back and forth to the Glenrose regularly for therapy, even after the three-month mark when I was officially discharged. I made a point of seeing Jerry every time I was there. One day, as I tottered down one of the hospital corridors on my crutches, a nurse called out to me.

"Hi, John," she said. "Where are you off to?"

"I'm just heading down to see Jerry between physio sessions."

The nurse put down the chart she was holding and walked toward me. "John, I'm sorry. I guess you couldn't have known—Jerry died last week."

I remember that clear as a bell. I was sad for Jerry, of course, but still glad I'd been bold enough to introduce him to Jesus. I heard little echoes, in that moment, of the situation with my friend Lionel all those years before, whom I had never spoken to about Jesus when he expressed fear about his upcoming surgery. But this time I'd chosen the right response. Jerry's last few months of life were still excruciatingly difficult, but they were far more restful and peaceful than they would have been had he not been able to lean on Jesus through his loneliness and pain. In fact, Jerry had always been learning, always asking questions, and always soaking up spiritual knowledge like a sponge. Even in the midst of our own lives, going through such chaos, feeling like everything was falling apart, there were little God moments like this that popped up every now and again.

*   *   *   *

Brent was responding well to treatment. His scalp wound was healing and his leg seemed to have set well enough that the medical staff took him out of traction and put him in a body cast.

Because I knew Brent was recovering well, I focused my energies on Byron. Early on in our hospital stint, one of John's sisters approached me in the hallway outside Brent's room with a book in her hand.

"Lorraine, I was thinking it might be good for you to read to Brent," she said to me.

Read to him? I barely had enough energy to hold the book up, let alone read it out loud and engage in high-energy banter with our six-year-old son and his active mind; I knew Brent was surrounded by family, so I wanted to use whatever energy I had to support my other son, whose condition was still hanging in the balance.

I gave a quick explanation about why I couldn't read to Brent as I carried on to Byron's room; I was sure my sister-in-law would understand, although as I headed down the hall I thought she'd looked at me a bit quizzically while we were speaking. Years later, as I better understood everything Brent had dealt with, I saw that this was the start of a journey of abandonment for him, although I wasn't aware of it at the time.

As time marched on, fewer friends popped in, but family members were still alongside us in the hospital. Brent's room was a natural gathering place for family because the atmosphere was so much more positive there. He was happy and healthy as he recovered, a typical six-year-old boy despite the head wound and broken leg, and he always seemed to have an aunt or uncle close at hand. Both my family and John's would check on Byron, stop by to chat with John for a bit, and then spend time with Brent. I was glad they were there, and—in the back of my mind—their constant attention made up for the amount of time I spent away from Brent, focused on Byron.

After about three weeks, Brent was the next one released. Now wearing a body cast and walking with crutches, he was eager to enjoy the fresh air and familiar surroundings of home turf. One of my friends from my nursing days, along with one of John's aunts, felt sorry for Brent during his hospital stay, and they'd bring him home-made soups or other fantastic meals. Sometimes they'd stop and pick up something from McDonald's they knew he'd like. By the time he was discharged, Brent was definitely not suffering from the skin-and-bones syndrome that afflicted so many others who were in hospital for long recovery periods!

Upon release, it was decided that Brent would stay with my parents. My brother Allen and his wife Louise lived on the same farm as my parents, and their little girls were Brent's constant companions. In the midst of those agonizing months of separation, with three of us still in the city, those little cousins were Brent's one slice of normal life.

Because of the seriousness of Byron's condition, Brent had not actually seen his brother during the initial hospital stay. While still in traction, Brent had had an early visit with John when the hospital staff wheeled Brent's bed, with its pulley and traction apparatus in place, up to John's nursing station. The staff put John's bedside next to Brent's in the hallway and the two of them connected by holding hands and talking briefly. We knew it was important for Brent to connect with his dad, but we hadn't wanted to traumatize him by showing him the full extent of his brother's condition. Nine-year-old Byron had always been six-year-old Brent's hero, and we weren't sure how Brent would react to seeing Byron comatose. Deep down, I'd hoped Byron would wake up soon, and that Brent could reconnect with his brother in some more normal way, but as Brent's release drew near and no apparent change occurred in Byron, we knew it would be important for Brent to see him, regardless of his condition. So, before we sent Brent off to stay with my parents, we brought him in to see Byron.

"C'mon in, Brent," I said to him as he manoeuvred himself through the doorway. I could see the excitement in Brent's eyes as he came in—at long last, he was going to see his hero brother again.

I stepped over to Byron's bed and adjusted the covers quickly. After three weeks in a coma, his body was starting to curl together and tighten up from disuse. At that point, one of his legs was pulled down and the other was crossed over on top of it, being pulled in another direction.

When I turned back to Brent, he was gone. I couldn't find him anywhere. I poked my head out into the hallway, but he wasn't there. I pulled doors away from the wall, thinking he might have ducked behind one, and I looked into the little bathroom annex, but Brent was nowhere to be seen. Finally, I found him over by the window—he had twirled himself into the long curtain and was crying.

"What's wrong, Brent?" I put my hand on his head and gently pulled him close for a hug. His hair was still quite bristly, just starting to grow back after being shaved, and tears were coursing down his tender little cheeks.

"Byron isn't like he used to be," Brent quivered, pushing his face against me. I just held him. I could sense all the fears and questions I had as an adult now hitting home with Brent, forever changing his relationship with his older brother—and shifting his whole foundation as to where he stood in the world. My heart broke all over again.

In that moment, it suddenly became very difficult for me to go through with the plan we'd worked out for Brent with my parents, but I knew it was the only option. Brent loved his grandparents, and their love for him was equally deep. We knew my parents would give Brent the care and attention he needed, and because he'd have the freedom to make his way over to Allen and Louise's to play with the girls, we knew Brent would have the closest thing possible to a normal six-year-old life while we continued to walk out our healing journey. Even knowing that, it was hard to put him in my parents' car that day and watch him drive away.

Seeds of abandonment were again being sown into Brent's young life.

Months passed as Brent returned to school and carried on a somewhat normal life. "Somewhat normal" meant he spent his days encased in the body cast, which prevented him from taking part in most activities. My family took good care of him, but the trauma was too much for his young mind to process. The details of those twelve months have been filed away deep in Brent's subconscious mind, and to this day he has little memory of that year.

The months passed, his cast was removed, and a short period of therapy ensued. Bit by bit, our little boy returned to a normal childhood—or the closest thing it could be for him.

Musings

CHAPTER 5

SILENCE DEAFENS

Back in Edmonton, another change was about to take place. Upon my initial arrival in the city, Jack and Carol Klemke had opened their home to me, enabling me to live nearby to the hospital. They even gave me a car to use so I didn't have to rely on anyone else to get around.

Jack and Carol Klemke were a remarkable source of stability and care for us. The Bible talks about the difference between folks who say the right things and people who actually do the right things, and the Klemkes were definitely people who were doers and not just talkers.

Initially, I assumed I'd be with the Klemkes for two or three weeks while John and the boys recovered, but time stretched slowly onward, becoming a month, and then three months.

As my stay with them reached the three-month mark, it became obvious that physical recovery, and hence our stay in the city, was going to take more time than any of us had guessed. I didn't want to overstay my welcome with the Klemkes, so I found an apartment in a building called the Hys Centre, connected by tunnel to the hospital.

I often think about Jack and Carol. John and I felt like God had gone silent; yet the Klemkes were a constant illustration of God's love in action. When others were quick to offer advice, believe it or not, on why we'd gotten into this mess and how to fix it, the Klemkes were simply there for us, taking any fuzzy notions of some ethereal God floating around somewhere and turning those instead into real and tangible expressions of concern and help. They took the abstract and put skin on it, showing me a real God with real love, offering genuine support during my darkest hours.

I use that as one of the measuring posts in my life today: am I living love, or am I just talking about it? Am I offering real service and help to people who need it, using whatever resources I have on hand to make a difference, or am I content to offer only empty words?

When I moved out of the Klemke home, there was no subtle sense of relief from them that now I'd be out of their hair; they seemed genuinely sad that I'd no longer be part of their day-to-day family life. I felt like I'd become a daughter in the Klemke household, and I treasure that as one of the bright lights in those dark days. It had certainly not felt like three months had passed since I was first welcomed into their home.

But it *had* been three months, and the changing seasons were evident every time I made my brief daily journey to the hospital. Winter was giving way to spring, and everywhere I looked I saw evidence of life coming back to the world: tulips and daffodils poked their way out of dead-looking flowerbeds, brittle brown twigs sported fresh green buds, and the cold bite of winter had disappeared from the air.

While my senses were aware of life returning to the world around me, my spirit still carried the heaviness of seeing none of that re-emerging life in Byron. Every day I'd return faithfully to his bedside, hoping against hope for noticeable improvement, yet every day I'd see his little body, devoid of muscle tone, continue to curl in on itself.

We'd been told right from that first week after the crash that Byron had sustained brain injury. Even as a former nurse, that had been very hard for me to process. I first heard the prognosis over the phone when I was in Whitecourt. The neurosurgeon shared his findings with me and explained that with the extent of brain injury Byron had suffered we could expect him to be spastic.

I knew what spastic meant, but in my post-traumatic mindset the only thing I could connect to was the memory of an acquaintance who'd had cerebral palsy and wore leg braces attached to brown leather shoes. My mind made the leap from the doctor's comment about being spastic to the picture of the leg braces, and I blurted out, "You mean he'll have to wear those brown shoes?"

I don't know if the neurosurgeon even knew what I meant, but he simply said, "Could be."

Even knowing he'd likely be spastic, I longed for my little Byron to come back to us. And nothing was happening.

Now on my own, I settled into a daily routine of rising early, engaging in contemplative Bible reading and devotional time, and then walking over to the hospital to spend the day with Byron and John. Even though God appeared to be silent—almost oblivious—to what was going on in our lives, I was determined to carry on with the spiritual disciplines that had been part of my life since I'd been a little girl. Having regular Bible-reading time every morning helped give me a sense of stability in the midst of a world gone mad.

One spring morning in my apartment I started my day as always, with Bible reading, reflection, and prayer. The scriptures I read told the story of Jesus dealing with a man who had leprosy. In Bible times, people with leprosy were outcasts and banned from society. In this instance, the man approached Jesus and said, "If you are willing, you could make me well."

"I am willing," Jesus said, and then he stretched out his hand and touched the man. The touch itself was unusual, because people with leprosy were avoided at all costs. "Be healed," Jesus said, and the man was cured.

I felt unsettled, maybe even agitated, as I closed the Bible. How many times had I read similar descriptions in the Bible about Jesus healing people? It seemed to occur time after time, page after page. And yet my little nine-year-old was across the street, lying in a hospital room, unable to connect with the world around him. Every day I prayed for him, and every day nothing happened. Every day!

I finished getting ready for the day and headed over to the hospital. This time, instead of first popping in to see Byron, I headed directly to John's room.

"I don't know why I even read the Bible," I blurted out when I saw him. "It's not true."

Needless to say, this was not the way I regularly greeted John. He looked at me for a bit, and then started asking questions. I poured out my pain, confusion, and disappointment at how nothing seemed to be changing for Byron, no matter how hard or how often we prayed. I could tell by the expression on John's face that he understood these pent-up emotions and the unanswerable questions. He empathized like no one else could.

Our church family had been very supportive throughout our ordeal. People came to visit and pray. When it became clear that Byron wouldn't regain consciousness anytime soon, the elders—the board of directors of the church—agreed to come pray for him. John and I read the Bible, and we believed what it said—to the point where we were willing to make decisions based on what we read. The Bible says that if someone is sick, they should call the church leaders together to pray and anoint them with oil. The Bible also says that believing-prayer will heal us if we're sick, and that Jesus will put us on our feet again. That was exactly the situation we were facing with Byron, so we were encouraged that these leaders were willing to step forward and walk with us in this.

In his characteristically assertive way, John told the elders that he didn't want anyone participating who didn't believe God could or would heal Byron. This was a solemn event, he explained, and there was no room for doubt.

The elders voluntarily chose to fast before gathering to pray; they wanted to be as prepared as possible. When they came in and gathered as a group, there was a real sense that God was in the room with us. As the prayer started, I closed my eyes and pressed in to add my own thoughts and prayers to those of the leaders who had come to stand with us in this critical time.

I could feel the faith rising in me as we carried on. We knew these leaders were committed to stand with us. As each man prayed, I could feel their faith starting to affect the atmosphere of the room; peace came in, a sense of God's love filled the place, and the usual mood of dread and ill-health lifted.

I was so thankful. I knew we were together in our prayers, and I knew God had heard us. I'd felt the shift in my own heart from discouragement to excitement as I thought about what God was about to do. This was amazing!

The spoken prayer came to a close, and I could feel the anticipation. I dared to open my eyes, barely a squint at first, and then wide open, certain that I would find Byron grinning back at me, mischievous eyes sparkling with delight, ready to jump up.

Nothing had happened.

Byron's body was still stooped over, secured by a belt into the wheelchair in which he'd been placed that morning.

All of us in the room, I think, were holding our breath, watching to see if there was going to be some stirring from Byron, some sign that he had been healed.

There was still nothing. It was heart-rending. Byron stayed just as he had been.

A few at a time, the leaders stood and made their way to the edge of the little circle we had formed. Some of the men walked closer to Byron's chair before leaving the circle, while others squeezed my shoulder or patted John's hand. It was awkward for anyone to speak, although a few of the men quietly uttered phrases such as, "We'll keep praying," or "Maybe it'll take a little time…" I was crushed, and I could tell most of these faithful friends were hard hit as well.

I remember looking at John. His eyes were closed, but I could see the tears spilling onto his cheeks. Despite doing everything exactly the way the Bible said, and even though we knew the leaders who had joined us were strong in their faith and as expectant as we were, as far as we could see our little boy had not been healed. I wept uncontrollably for some time.

*　　*　　*　　*

Lorraine and I had shared such a strong conviction that God would come through, that our little nine-year-old would snap out of his coma and jump back to full health. The complete lack of evidence of anything having happened hammered both of us deeply.

Not long after the prayer session, we were visited by Jim Mabbot, the physician who had seen fit to take us under his wing. He was the one who had helped me find my bearings again, and I don't know if he was even aware of it.

"You know, John and Lorraine, I've been thinking about that prayer time you and the leaders from your church had for Byron," said Jim. "I know medical people, and if Byron had been healed in that moment, it would have been amazing—but everyone would have forgotten about it in a couple of days."

I knew I wouldn't have forgotten it, but I listened to what he was saying.

"As it is now, though, all the hospital staff are simply watching your response to life's harsh realities. You're under the microscope, and it's speaking volumes to these medical personnel."

I hadn't considered that before. Jim perhaps didn't know the impact he was making with his off-the-cuff remarks, but it certainly reminded me that there is always a bigger picture in play. I do not believe God caused the wreck, nor do I believe God left Byron apparently unhealed simply as an object lesson to those around us, but being told people were watching us reminded me that there's often a perspective beyond our own—and that God's reality of what was happening in our lives included aspects outside of our immediate perception. In other words, what we were seeing was not always the full picture of what was actually happening.

That really helped me get back on my feet, metaphorically speaking, and I was again able to stand on what I already believed about God from His past record. In regard to my unwritten tomorrows, I was able to write that in as a foundational value: *What I see happening is not always the full picture of what's really going on.*

* * * *

So it was that when I came into John's room and declared that the Bible wasn't true, John and I talked about what had gone wrong. I think I just needed to vent, because I was tired of always looking on the bright side and trying to maintain my faith. It was really getting to me that God was so glaringly and obviously silent. John listened, asked a few questions, and let me go on dumping out my pain. He listened, we dialogued, and he held my hand.

Then he shifted in his bed and looked at me. "Before the elders came that day, I was convinced God would heal Byron," he said. "I remember sitting here in this room, thinking about God and how good He is—I was sure He would heal Byron!" He squeezed my hand. "When Byron wasn't healed in that moment, it really rocked my world. It hit me harder than dealing with my own injuries and recovery, and I'm still not sure which way is up."

John's eyes met mine again, and I could see complete authenticity in them.

"But you know, Lorraine," he said, "regardless of what I see, I'm going to choose to believe."

I thought about what John said as I walked to Byron's room, and for a long time afterward. I sat by my son's bed and gazed out the window while I processed everything. I knew for certain I'd seen God act before; I recalled the little adventure Byron and I had shared the year previously with the cheque blowing in the wind. I also knew that sometimes bad things just happened. I knew God didn't pick sides, but somehow, deep down, I thought we deserved better treatment.

Had I subconsciously believed I was entitled to something better? Even though I wouldn't have said it out loud, if I was honest with myself I'd have to say I thought, at least to some extent, that if we were living according to what God and the Bible said, we would somehow be spared the worst of things—but now I wasn't so sure where that thought really came from. Was I thinking of God only as a father figure, ready to protect me whenever someone else made a bad choice that affected me or my family—like the man who chose to drive drunk on New Year's Day? I knew that was unrealistic—but had it been what I believed deep down inside?

On the other hand, the Bible *did* say that Jesus healed people, and that if sick people had the elders pray over them they'd get better.

I didn't know where that left me. All I knew for sure was that, despite how involved we'd been spiritually, our understanding up to that point of who He was and how He related to us was shallow. And it wouldn't get any deeper for me if I gave up now.

I got out my Bible the next morning, the same as every morning, and kept reading from where I'd left off the day before. From that point forward, I started journaling in the margins of my Bible; when I came across something during my reading that challenged my faith, I would take my pen and write a little comment. Then I would date it and write the phrase, "I stand on Your Word."

* * * *

I was a very driven young man leading up to the car crash. Not content with merely being "Mr. Ordinary," I dove into life and business head-on, determined to be highly successful in every endeavour.

Sometimes I think my drivenness was at least partially a result of growing up the youngest boy with four older sisters who were phenomenally successful in school. Right from Grade One, it seemed that each of my teachers compared me to one or more of my sisters. The comparison was never favourable toward me! It was quite a legacy for a scruffy little boy to live up to. The inner vow that said "Yeah? Well I'll show them!" was never far from my mind once I hit my teen years. That inner drive persisted into adulthood.

I took a stab at politics early on, but when I didn't win, I didn't think of it as a setback; I learned everything I could from the process and used the contacts and networks I'd built to continually push my business interests forward.

It seemed that Lorraine and I experienced a degree of success everywhere we turned in those early years. We had strong faith in God, the ability to bring the right people onto the team, and a hardy work ethic to keep us focused and moving forward. We plugged into a church, too, serving as leaders, doing what we could to make the church relevant in its community. Life was good, life was full, and life was centered on God.

The years leading up to the crash had been full of incredible and truly out-of-the-ordinary business opportunities for me—some the result of a lot of hard work, and others that seemed to simply fall into my lap.

One of the long and slowly built opportunities I took involved one of Canada's last privately-held trust companies, a genuine savings and loan institution. Canada's banking system is different than that of the United States; all the major players are national (and international) in scope, with huge centralized banks that have branches in virtually every city and town across the country.

But here was a great opportunity, indeed: a genuine, privately owned trust company looking for new ownership. Controlled by one family since its inception, this savings and loan company had weathered financial storms in the past and was standing strong and secure, kind of like Bailey Savings and Loan in *It's a Wonderful Life*.

Having dealt with banks all my life, sometimes feeling like they were the ones that held all the power over my ability to move forward and expand in business, I jumped at the chance of putting myself in the driver's seat, so to speak.

My early conversations with the trust company's president, Andrew Hirschell, revealed him to be an astute and thoughtful businessman, one who was proud of the family heritage his company represented. Hirschell told me his son had moved to New York to pursue plans of his own—plans that did not include becoming next in the family line of trust company presidents and owners.

The time had come for Hirschell to call it quits. Closing the operation down as he approached retirement was not an option, and he wanted to ensure that his "baby" would pass into good hands.

I spent more than eighteen months building a strong portfolio of private investors who were willing to join in the acquisition of this company. I worked out a strong proposal. I met with people, wrote lengthy and persuasive letters, and spent countless hours on the phone. Slowly but surely the plan came together, and the money I needed to swing this deal gradually began flowing in.

With our financing established, we were now closing in on the actual acquisition. With a year and a half of work under my belt, I flew to the company's headquarters to meet with Hirschell and finalize our deal.

We met in Hirschell's office and went through all the necessary paperwork. The final details on the table were relatively simple matters: timelines, employee transitions, things of that nature. A team of lawyers waited in the outer office, literally on hold until we concluded our final discussions.

As we talked, the elderly gentleman kept bringing up stories of successes and failures over the years, things his father had done, things his grandfather before him had done. Some of the stories were quite humorous, and he would chuckle as he ran his fingers through his white hair. His eyes, though, would then turn thoughtful behind his glasses. I could tell it was hard for him to see the business leave the family.

Just as we were moving to the final signing, Hirschell leaned back in his chair, paused, and reached for the phone.

"Excuse me, John," he said as he dialled. "I just have to make a quick call."

I was surprised at the interruption, but I, too, leaned back and waited for him to finish. I understood that this was probably the biggest transition he'd ever faced in his life, so I was willing to brush aside my own eagerness for things to be concluded in order to give him a chance to process things a bit.

"Hey, son," he said into the phone. I could hear his son's voice faintly as he responded to his dad. "Let me get right to the point. We've talked a lot lately, and you know that I've been making plans to sell the company." Hirschell glanced at me over his glasses while he continued talking into the phone. "Son, I'm asking you to come home from New York City. If you don't, this family-owned company will be gone by tonight."

I could hear the silence on the New York end of the line. And I was in shock at what I had just heard Hirschell ask his son.

Then I heard the son say something.

"Okay son, we'll talk later."

Hirschell hung up and turned back to me.

"He's coming home. Sorry, John, the deal is off." Hirschell stood, but it took me forever to get out of my chair. I could not believe what had just transpired! A year and a half of work! All that money raised! The whole deal gone, just like that!

This was a devastating blow, even though other than a few travel expenses and some lawyer's fees it hadn't really cost me much. I was seriously disappointed.

But I was young, I had many other things to focus on, and I was sure something else would come up; it wasn't the end of the world.

Something else did come up. Another wonderful opportunity that year seemed to fall out of the sky into my lap, dropping in when we were away from home in Scottsdale, Arizona. We had a second home there, a place we could visit whenever we felt we needed a break.

I was in our Scottsdale kitchen one November morning, glancing through the Phoenix paper while I enjoyed a cup of coffee. The phone rang; the caller was a man named Arlis, an older man we knew from his role as an executive with an international Christian organization. He was a man I respected, a savvy businessman, well-experienced, and someone who had a heart for spiritual matters. I was still young at the time and he was much older than I was, but we'd hit it off nonetheless and become good friends.

Arlis was well-known and well-respected in the larger corporate community, too. By the time I knew him, he'd already been called to the White House several times for meetings, and had even served as an advisor to one of the U.S. presidents.

Today's phone call, though, wasn't about presidential advice. It was about farming.

"John, I'd like you to come with me for the day, if you've got time," he said.

"I could do that, Arlis. Why? What's up?"

"Well, I'm one of two owners of a large cotton farm in southwest Phoenix. I was intrigued by your operation up in Canada when I last visited, and I was hoping you could come by so I could show you our operation here."

I thought it was a good idea, so I took my nine-year-old son Byron along with me for the day. We had a lot of fun together.

Arlis showed us through the entire operation, a large cotton farm with more than 180 employees. Byron and I were shown how the field operations worked, how the cotton was gathered and then processed, and how they prepared it to be shipped to market. Each stage of the cotton's journey from field to market required some pretty significant machinery, and my nine-year-old and I had a lot to keep us interested throughout the day.

"Well, John, what do you think?" asked Arlis as the day wore to a close. We were sitting in a restaurant drinking coffee while Byron enjoyed a milkshake. I told Arlis how impressed I was by the size of the farm and the number of people it took to keep things running.

"However, I've got to tell you, Arlis, that I don't think the operation as a whole is running as well as it could be." I watched his face, trying to gauge whether this information was something he wanted to hear or not. He stayed steady, so I pressed further. "In fact, it's pretty bad."

Arlis looked at me for a moment and then smiled. "Well, John, that's why I asked you here. I was pretty sure you'd see things that way."

I must have looked confused, because Arlis chuckled to himself.

"John, I know it's not running all that well. And I know that needs to change. Here's my idea: why don't you buy a third of the farm, and then run the company? That'd straighten things out!"

I was intrigued. The farm already turned a profit, but I could see it being much more efficient, and therefore more profitable if it was run better. I knew we could get the farm running as well as the one back home, and with the market that existed for cotton I knew this was a good opportunity.

Arlis and I talked a bit longer. I asked a lot of questions, and he gave me a lot of answers—answers I liked.

"Hey, John, I haven't told you who the other partner is yet," Arlis exclaimed at one point. "My partner, who would become your partner, too, is Roy Rogers."

"The horse-riding Roy Rogers?"

"That's right," said Arlis. "Roy Rogers and Dale Evans own the other half of this farm. And if you decide to sign on, they'll fly out here tomorrow night, we'll have dinner together, and then we'll sign all the papers."

I must have looked a little flabbergasted.

"I've already talked with my lawyer and my banker," he told me. "Everything is lined up, and the bank'll front you any financing you need. We're ready to move on this if you are."

Man, was I excited! Not only was it a great business opportunity, but I'd be in partnership with Roy Rogers and Dale Evans! For a kid who grew up on a farm, it doesn't get much better than that!

I told Arlis that I was almost one hundred percent ready to sign up, and Byron and I dashed back to Scottsdale to share the news with Lorraine. Knowing her reserved personality, during the short drive back I thought through several scenarios that might win her approval.

Back in Scottsdale I called Bill, our lead farmhand, to talk about the situation. I knew how important he was to our operation back home, but I also knew we wouldn't be able to get the Arizona farm up to peak efficiency without his help. Would he consider moving here to take this farm in hand, even for just a couple of years? I could hardly wait for Bill to call me back.

"My wife and I have chatted about it, John, and we agree that it's a great opportunity," Bill told me. "Our kids are nowhere near school age yet, so we could probably stay down in Arizona for up to five years if we needed to. You can count me in."

I was ecstatic! Everything was coming together on a wonderful business opportunity! I'd be in partnership with Arlis, Roy Rogers, and Dale Evans, and to top it all off we'd be having dinner with the famous duo the following night. I went to bed a happy man.

But when I awoke the next morning, I felt disturbed and agitated; it took me a while to realize that the source of my restlessness was the impending deal. I sat on the edge of our bed, turning things over and over in my mind. Was there something I'd missed? Some detail I'd overlooked that God was trying to draw my attention to?

I headed to the kitchen to grab a coffee and talk about it with Lorraine.

"You know, John," said Lorraine, "it might be possible that the deal is as good as you think it is, but God is just trying to tell you it's not the right time for it."

As soon as she said it, I knew Lorraine was right. And I hated to admit it. I'd been looking forward to this potential partnership with Roy Rogers and Dale Evans, and I knew the cotton farm would be a significant profit maker when it was running right. But I also knew this lack of peace was something I had to take seriously.

I called Arlis with the disappointing news.

"You're not serious, John, are you?" he said after I'd explained what was going on.

"I don't know what to say, Arlis. I just know that this lack of peace is significant, and I think God may be telling me to say no to the offer at this time. And Lorraine has no peace about the venture, either."

"Well, John, you realize Roy and Dale aren't going to fly in to have dinner with us if there is no deal, don't you?"

"Yes, Arlis, I realize that," I said. "I really wanted to meet them, and I really wanted to partner with all of you in this—but I need to respect what I think God is telling me."

"Very well, John, I understand and appreciate that," said Arlis. "I'd best get on the phone to Roy and tell him about the change in plans. Bye now, but let's chat again before you head back up to Canada." We both hung up.

And that was that. My opportunity to partner with Roy Rogers and Dale Evans, and to own part of a great cotton farm with my friend Arlis, closed as quickly as it had opened.

It wasn't until years later that I realized how wise God had been in that whole season, even though I couldn't see then what He was up to. The cotton farm opportunity had dropped into our laps less than six weeks before the New Year's Day car wreck, and the trust company would have been transitioning to our ownership at about the same time. If we'd been extended in all those directions when we were taken out of commission—and if we'd had Bill focused on the Arizona operation rather than our home farm—we would probably not have survived either relationally or financially.

Be that as it may, my drive to succeed remained with me over the months of my recovery, both in and out of hospital. Business had been a challenge, obviously, and Lorraine had taken on a huge role throughout my recovery. During my hospital stay, she'd fly home every week to check on the company finances, check on the farm, check on various aspects of the business, meet with lawyers, bankers, and key staff members, collect any necessary papers I'd need to sign, and then fly back to rejoin Byron and me at the hospital.

I was the third member of our family to be discharged.

Once I was discharged, even though I still had years of physical rehabilitation ahead, I knew it would simply be a matter of getting myself back in the saddle, hunkering down, and pushing forward in business. I was convinced it would only be a matter of time until we had regained any momentum we'd lost, and I was confident our financial situation would be back on track in the not-too-distant future.

Brent and I were carving out a new lifestyle with just the two of us at home. I was gradually getting back to my business interests, and a bit of the old energy was returning. But it was all happening so much slower than I had hoped.

One day, Brent and I were out in the yard. It was springtime the year following the crash, and at long last Brent was out of his body cast and able to scoot around like any other seven-year-old. I was still hobbling around on two canes, but it certainly felt good to be out in the fresh air as winter slipped away.

Brent was tearing around in the yard exploring all the fun places he hadn't been able to make much use of during the weeks when he was encased in plaster. He clambered up into the boys' tree fort and called down for me to join him up there.

"I can't get up there, Brent," I called back to him. "I'll stay here on the ground."

I felt as warm and fresh on the inside as the day was on the outside, just watching Brent reconnect with his childhood. Lassie, the boys' German Shepherd, joined in the excitement as she ran barking around the base of the tree fort.

"You know, Dad, I'm finally starting to get my life back together again," Brent said from his vantage point in the fort; I could see he had seated himself and was gazing out over his backyard domain.

As humorous as that phrase sounded coming from a seven-year-old, the words rang true, and they encouraged my heart. No more body cast for Brent, no more being tied down. In years to come, Brent would find himself dealing with other weighty issues, but in that moment he was a little boy simply enjoying being a little boy.

There was something fresh going on, and it felt great. Perhaps the only thing that had shifted was our own understanding, but we definitely had a much greater appreciation for the fact that we were utterly and completely dependent upon God for everything in our lives. We were at such a new place, however, that even though we were seeing God show up time and time again, it still seemed like a surprise when He did.

Musings

CHAPTER 6

SILENCE AMPLIFIES

Byron's recovery took him from a drug-induced coma to a natural coma, and at some point to a place of unawareness that was no longer defined as coma. To us, the line that separated one from the other was unclear. In our desperation to nudge him out of his nonresponsive state, we began to schedule weekend trips to take Byron home to familiar surroundings. Still, none of the stories that gave us hope—miraculous accounts of comatose people suddenly waking up—became his reality. Byron's emergence was a slow, challenging journey to awareness. He was locked inside a body that could not respond appropriately.

My weekends at home during Byron's rehabilitation were nothing like my weekends before the crash. Rather than having time off, I worked harder than ever. I'd lift Byron into the car at the hospital, load his chair, drive five hours home, care for Byron around the clock, reconnect with Brent and John, take care of business responsibilities, clean the house, wash clothes, and make meals for the next week. I also prepared a noon meal for family and friends who cared for Byron on Sunday mornings while we went to church. It was a "thank you" to everyone who'd been helping us, but it was extra work. As much work as it all was, though, I was glad to see Byron in familiar surroundings: I was willing to try anything that might bring him back to us.

My parents did whatever they could to help. Early that summer, my mom and dad started driving Byron back the three hundred miles to the city hospital and staying with him every second week. That allowed me to actually stay home for a stretch and support John and Brent.

I recall one week when I was doing the driving. I'd made a Sunday dinner, as was our custom, sharing our table with all who'd helped with Byron and the family. The meal included roast chicken, one of our favourites, and somehow my dad got a chicken bone stuck in his throat. He wasn't choking, and he wasn't in pain, but somehow the bone had become lodged and stuck, and no amount of mashed potatoes or other food would wash it down.

We finished the meal, cleaned the dishes, and I prepared for my trip back with Byron. My dad was still in some discomfort because of the bone in his throat, but he insisted he was fine, so John helped me lift Byron into the car and we headed off on our long drive back to the city.

Upon our arrival at the hospital some six hours later, a nurse helped me settle Byron back in his room.

"Mrs. Baergen," said the nurse as we finished getting Byron into bed, "your father is on this floor, too, if you'd like to pop in and see him before you leave for the night."

My father?

It turned out he'd stopped in at our local hospital to have the bone-in-craw situation checked after Byron and I had left town. The physician on-call that evening felt it was serious enough for my dad to be airlifted to the city hospital. He'd been transported and admitted between when I'd left home and arrived in the city. Once we knew he was actually okay, we all got quite a laugh upon finding out that he was just down the hallway and through the double doors.

During the recovery phase, we received a lot of "helpful" comments and advice from people trying to speak into our situation. Two incidents stand out in my mind as typifying the ways in which people would bring their thoughts and opinions to us.

One older lady, who'd known our family for years, said she knew precisely what had caused our misfortune. At one Sunday evening meeting, she laid her hand on my arm, gently pulled me away from everyone else, and said, "Lorraine, I know you're carrying a load."

I couldn't argue with that. I was tired beyond belief and still had to pack later that evening to return Byron to the hospital.

"I know you've prayed a great deal about this," the woman continued, "and I have been praying, too." The woman laid her hand on my arm again and looked me straight in the eye. "I believe God is not healing Byron because you wear earrings."

I was stunned! The woman prattled on, but I no longer listened. However bizarre they were, her comments still stung. I didn't believe God operated that way, nor did I think something we'd done as individuals or as a family had caused this tragedy. The sting came from the fact that here, in my church—the one place where I should feel safe and loved—I'd been judged, and ridiculously so.

I realized, of course, that this woman didn't speak for everyone in the church. I knew she was probably trying to help—probably trying to steer me back onto the straight and narrow so God would see fit to step in and heal Byron. But even after telling myself those things, I became less willing to expose myself emotionally for fear of getting more "helpful" advice. The result? I avoided her. What if she noticed I was wearing nail polish? What about my lipstick; would that spark more speculation?

By evading her, though, I fell into agreement with the enemy. I concluded that people her age and in her stage of life wouldn't, and maybe couldn't, understand me. Unknowingly, I built a wall of protection around myself, a buffer against her and people like her.

The other incident of not-so-helpful advice occurred at home. Living as we did on a farm, there was plenty of property around the house. One weekend I was surprised to see a large motor home pulling off the road into our driveway.

As I watched, the motor home found itself a place in the yard and settled in, much like a large dog that circles the living room carpet and finds the perfect place to curl up in the sun. John wasn't home, so I invited the couple in. I remembered them from my childhood days. While I finished making lunch, we talked briefly, reacquainting ourselves.

After John arrived, we had lunch together. As we talked, it became clear why they'd come: their own son had suffered a catastrophic brain injury as a two-year-old. Having heard of our situation, they felt compelled to help. It was obvious they cared, and we could tell they understood pain.

They offered to help in practical ways, and they promised not to bother us. I knew this gesture came from their hearts, and was prompted by their personal experience, but as we talked I started to realize the conversation was somewhat one-sided. They'd agonized over their son, it was true, but they assumed every detail of our experience mirrored theirs. Despite my misgivings, I welcomed their assistance, given that our family, friends, and acquaintances were starting to drift back into their own routines. This couple might just give us the help we still so desperately needed.

After only a short time, though, I noticed tension building between them and us. They seemed unwilling, or unable, to meet us in our unique need—it was like they had their own agenda.

After following me around the house for several hours, chattering constantly and giving advice, the woman came to the kitchen where I was working, closed the door behind her, and asked me to sit with her at the table. Given her tone throughout the day, I was pretty sure I knew what she was about to say.

"What's up?" I asked.

"Well, Harold and I have been talking, and we believe we need to tell you something."

I said nothing. I was sure she didn't realize how intrusive her presence had been, and she seemed oblivious to my aloofness toward her. It was clear she had no feeling for Byron; she hadn't taken the time to get to know him or his rightful place in our family.

"Harold and I believe you're doing the wrong thing for your family."

I had no idea what she was trying to say, so I just listened.

"We think you should put Byron into an institution," she explained. "It's obvious your workload is huge, and we believe you're making a mistake by keeping him at home with you."

I explained that this was something we'd already agreed upon, and that we were content to move forward with the strength and insight God was giving us. An institution was not an option.

I thought the matter was closed, but for the next few hours she continued to follow me around, challenging our decision. I finally reached the point where I'd had enough, and quietly stepped outside to speak with John. I found him in the shop working on a farm implement.

"John," I blurted, "I cannot take these people!" I explained what had been going on and said I could no longer handle the situation.

We talked for a bit, and then John squeezed my shoulder, grabbed his crutches, and headed to the motor home. He was going to ask them to leave.

By the time I got back to the house, I could see the couple packing up their gear. Without looking up at the house, they drove away.

I sincerely appreciated their desire to help, but once again I was floored by how it had actually played out. Like the earring lady's advice, their counsel was hollow and hurtful—it didn't reflect a genuine understanding or appreciation of us, or our situation.

What a contrast that was to the support we received from family and friends like our pastor, Del, who often spent time with us without saying a word.

I can see now how important it was for me to have a firm spiritual foundation upon which I could stand during those challenging times. I learned, albeit slowly, to rest in the certainty of whom I knew God to be.

Sometimes we fall into the trap of thinking, *If I'm living out of God's plan for me—if I'm doing what I think God is asking of me—then my life should get better and better.* But that line of thinking can become a setup for disaster, because when life becomes hard we have no frame of reference for processing the hard stuff. But for me, with all the preparation God had seen fit to give us, I was able to come to a place of recognizing that God can be trusted no matter what the circumstances are saying.

I've also learned that I don't have to have the answers for those around me who might find themselves in this dry no-man's land where nothing makes sense. Silence, in those times, speaks much louder than words.

But we tend to grasp for the answers. I've come to believe that needing to know "what's going on" is a way of being on top of the situation, of trying to stay in control. My ability to be in control of any situation quickly evaporates when one of the most constant prayers in my heart is "What's happening, God?" and there is no sense of a response being given.

I see it clearly now. Whether I feel peaceful or frantic depends on whether or not I give up control. If my anxiety levels rise, I know I'm leaning on my own ability to figure things out and fix them. In other words, I'm trusting in myself to the exclusion of anyone or anything else, putting my trust in my ability to fix things on my own. Then I'm drawn into a vicious cycle of not knowing what's happening, trying harder to fix it, but getting nowhere. On the other hand, when I'm peaceful, I know I'm resting in the truth that God sees the big picture, even though I don't. I may not know what's happening, but I trust Him and His plans for me.

Have I always trusted God and believed He was working to better our lives? Certainly not. It was a constant struggle, living in the tension between what we believed and what we saw in our daily lives. As our trust grew, it became possible to live in that tension. It's really a very basic faith question that's on the table in these times: is God good, and can He be trusted to have my best interests at heart? If my answer is yes, then I'm able to rest as I trust Him.

Despite having settled the trust question in my mind, the struggle of living in that tension was not settled quite as easily. It seemed to reappear when I faced the reality of what life had now become for us as a family.

*　*　*　*

I'd been out of the hospital for several months, although I was continuing my outpatient physiotherapy visits to the Glenrose.

By early September, the annual harvest of oats, wheat and canola was well underway. We'd begun swathing and combining, bringing our year's income out of the fields and into the granaries. Our grain fields were spread over a fifteen-mile radius, with large fields interspersed among those of our neighbours. It felt good to know our financial pressures would ease once we completed the harvest. I recalled God's intervention the previous year, when the canola crop had threatened to blow right out of the field. A lot had happened between that time and now, and as harvest season set in I started to get the sense that maybe everything was going to be okay.

Disaster struck with exquisite timing. Hail! No warning, and in a no-hail zone—right at crop maturity. If the grain was damaged, there'd be no growing season left for recovery.

It was midweek, and Lorraine was still with Byron in the hospital. As soon as the hailstorm passed, Bill and I headed out in different vehicles to check the crops. We could already see that the fields in the immediate vicinity were wiped out.

"What have you got, Bill?" I asked over the CB radio. I was just coming to our next field, and it looked bad.

"This first one's a goner," Bill said.

"This one on my side is, too. Let me know when you get to the next one."

I started noticing something strange as I drove past the in-between farm fields and arrived at our next field. I wondered if Bill was seeing anything like what I was seeing.

"Hey, John," I heard Bill's voice through the radio. "This is really weird."

It sounded like he was finding something out of the ordinary as well. "What is it, Bill?"

"Well, our field here is ruined just like the last one, but the MacPherson field between our last one and this one seems to be fine."

Bill was seeing the same thing I was.

"It's the same thing here," I said. "Our crops are destroyed, but the neighbours' land between our fields is untouched. I've never seen anything like it." The CB was silent. "Hey, drive out to the end of our land and see if it's like that all the way. I'm going to do the same in this direction."

"Okay, John, I'll do that. Let me know what you find."

Sure enough, as I drove down the highway to the farthest fields, I saw the same thing repeated time after time. In our fields, nothing remained standing; the hail had destroyed our crops. But land operated by our neighbours had received minimal damage.

When Bill and I arrived back at the main yard and compared notes, he told me the same story. Along the entire fifteen-mile stretch, our crops were either badly damaged or completely destroyed, while everyone else's seemed virtually untouched.

I'd heard stories about people praying and having their crops saved while everyone else's were ruined, like a shield of protection in the midst of destruction. But never had I heard of anything like this, where pockets of land were struck while surrounding parcels were preserved. In the language of modern warfare, it certainly looked like a "targeted hit."

So much for the growing sense that we'd be okay. The annihilation of a main source of income was more than a setback; it was a disaster. And added to the financial stress was my fear that any chance of returning to business life as I once knew it was slipping from my grasp. The death of that dream drained the very life out of me.

What could I do?

I continued to hang on, and my roots steadily grew deeper and stronger.

I could tell Lorraine was dealing with some of the same things. Previously, she'd served as controller in our four companies. She'd balanced work and her personal ministry to women with her roles as wife and mother. Now she was a constant caregiver, and I could see it was getting to her. Life's current realities were presenting her with difficult, sometimes dreaded, choices. Family, friendships, business... they'd all given way to our immediate needs.

Our tensions overlapped, and at the same time ran in different directions. We didn't have a lot of time together while Byron remained in hospital, and those few hours we did share over the weekends didn't leave a lot of time for sitting and talking casually. We did, however, keep our earlier commitment to pray together whenever possible. We kept that up even during this stress-filled period. I believe strongly that this choice, written earlier on in our life together, laid out a track we could run on and cling to during these unwritten and unplanned-for times of just hanging on.

I can see why divorce is so rampant in our society, even in situations where spouses have remained physically and emotionally faithful. Dealing with the stresses caused by extreme circumstances, such as the death of child or financial ruin—or, in our case, traumatic life-changing injuries—can destabilize the most solid of relationships. People in these situations can feel frightened, misunderstood, and alone in the darkness. Sometimes the fissure grows to the point where the relationship appears to be beyond recovery, and one or both parties make the choice to opt out. Hanging on, choosing to remain steady and committed during times of intense pressure, runs counter to the culture surrounding us.

All of us face pressures like this in our closest relationships at one point or another. Often it's not the seriousness of our circumstances that determines the degree of difficulty, but rather the intensity of our fear, misunderstanding, and isolation. In those times, hanging on can actually feel like the least sensible choice. And, yes, it *is* a choice. It's a choice walked out over minutes and hours and days and weeks.

All I know for sure is that the choice we'd made earlier, the choice to pray together every day, kept us deeply connected. When the pressures told us to let go—of our faith, of our marriage—we were able to hold each other and lean into Jesus together, because He had the strength we needed to keep hanging on.

*   *   *   *

The day of Byron's final discharge finally came! In preparation, we were asked to meet with one of the hospital psychologists, something that hadn't occurred when either Brent or John were discharged. Because we'd been anticipating the togetherness our official reunion as a family would bring, we'd brought Brent with us to the hospital. He joined us in the psychologist's office.

We sat in front of the doctor's wide desk and he took a few moments to shuffle through the open file before he spoke.

"Mr. and Mrs. Baergen, I see here that your son Byron is due to be released today."

We nodded, waiting to see what this was all about.

"According to what I have in the file here," said the doctor, "you haven't told us which institution you'd like to have Byron transported to."

John cleared his throat, but I was the first to speak. "We're taking him home, Doctor. We're not putting him in an institution."

The doctor looked at us both intently. "I have to tell you, Mr. and Mrs. Baergen, I think you're making the wrong decision. Byron is still not fully self-aware, and he will never recover beyond his current level."

We stared at the doctor. I felt Brent stir uncomfortably beside me, so I took his little hand in mine. The doctor continued.

"Let me be absolutely straight with you, Mrs. Baergen. You want to take Byron home with you because you do not want to lose him. I understand that. But you will lose him anyway."

Now I reached for John's hand as well.

"You'll lose him when you aren't able to give him the constant care he needs; we've seen this happen over and over again. You'll lose your husband, your marriage, and both your sons. The constant physical care Byron needs will quickly overwhelm you both, and when things get too tough you'll end up putting Byron in an institution anyway. And your second little boy here will have no opportunity for a normal life."

The doctor stood up and closed the file on his desk. It felt like he'd closed the file on our lives.

"Listen to me, Mr. and Mrs. Baergen. If you do not put your son Byron into an institution, you will lose each other and your younger son." He then dismissed us with a wave of his hand. "I'll leave you to think about that."

Words cannot express the heart-wrenching pain we felt at having to make such a monumental decision. And to complicate things, John and I were not on the same page about what we should be doing. How do you wrestle through these emotionally charged, values-impacting decisions when you can't fully understand and appreciate your partner's position? But, still, a decision now had to be made.

*　*　*　*

When the hospital psychologist told us we could lose everything, I was really taken aback. Lorraine and I had both known it would be a tough road to walk down, of course—although at that point neither of us had any idea how hard it would be. Lorraine had just accepted that as part of our new reality.

But I don't think I had realized the full weight of what we faced until the psychologist's words threw me into a tailspin. When we left his office, I remember Lorraine kneeling beside Brent, holding him close to her, saying, "Now, Brent, with us and Jesus we're going to make it."

I wasn't so sure.

We'd been preparing for this day a long time, but it had played out in a completely unexpected manner. Our emotions were all over the map, moving from excitement to huge concern to outright fear.

For the rest of the day, I found myself just going through the motions—loading Byron and his chair into the car, signing the final discharge papers, hitting the road to drive home—while internally I was pulling back into myself and sinking into a deep time of reflection. I needed that drive home for some serious "windshield time"—time to just sit and think about what was happening. There was little conversation as we made our way over the same stretch of road we had now travelled so many times since that fateful January day.

While Brent, Lorraine and I gradually turned the corner back to health, Byron remained locked away from us in a state of complete unawareness. Deep down, we wondered if Byron might somehow return to the boy he once was. We were convinced he was aware of more than he could communicate, but how much more, we didn't know.

I found myself thinking about Byron's potential. Our spunky, life-loving son had started hitting his stride before the accident, growing in maturity and vitality, embracing life with full enthusiasm. What would come of that? I kept picturing him as he had once been.

A slow but deep grieving for Byron began in me. It wasn't necessarily an outward grieving, nor was it something I was aware of every moment. Still, an undercurrent of sorrow for my little boy took root in me and became a constant companion for the ensuing weeks and months.

In my own personal recovery plan, in which I saw our forward momentum being rebuilt and our finances being restored, I'd thought mainly about my own role—my ability to take care of things, to focus, and to rise above the physical challenges that lay ahead. Throughout my physical recovery, I'd clung to thoughts of rebuilding and reengaging, looking forward to the day when we were all out of the hospital and I was free to fully embrace business life again. I hadn't fully considered the impact of Byron's condition and the constant care he'd require. Sure, I'd thought about it, but more in terms of assuming it was something Lorraine would do during the day while I was out rebuilding my business world.

The road before us seemed to change from one of opportunity and challenge to one that was bleak and empty, much like a forest landscape after a devastating fire. As melodramatic as it may sound, it truly felt like the suddenly charred remains of my dreams and plans were now smouldering on the scorched earth, and for the first time since the crash I found myself thinking that maybe everything wouldn't be okay after all.

Was this my new reality? Was my life now going to regress to settling for less? Were Lorraine and I going to merely exist, moving from one day to the next in a routine that would never change?

That whole month became a time of incredible wrestling for me. The walls started to close in, the load seemed to get heavier every day, and the hopelessness I felt dipped to new lows.

I found myself sinking into a deep chasm of self-pity. I did a lot of grumbling. I didn't notice it much myself—which I suspect is the case for most of us when we're trying to come to terms with something and our internal struggle leaks out into the surrounding environment—but I'm pretty sure others did. I thought I was just grumbling to myself, and maybe to God, but one day Lorraine took a long look at me and made an uncharacteristically strong statement.

"If you're not careful, you're going to lose your other son, too."

And I was pretty sure she meant much more than what her words conveyed.

Musings

CHAPTER 7

HANGING ON

Lorraine's bold words jolted me into reality. Had those words come from anyone else, I might have shrugged them off. But now I listened.

My dad's words, spoken just weeks before he died, came back with full impact. Although I didn't realize it at the time, I had watched my father live an example that would now help me. He had known what it was like to be held captive by past hurts; he had also experienced the freedom that came with putting those issues to rest.

In his later years, my father managed one of our businesses, a car wash. We were happy to have him, and he was glad to have a low-stress job that kept him busy during semi-retirement. He always had a Bible open on his desk, and when the car wash didn't need his steady hand or watchful eye, he'd spend his time reading and pondering.

I popped into his office one day and found him reading his ever-present Bible. These father-son times had become special—times when we'd chat about what Jesus was showing him. On this day, as we talked about the fresh insights he'd received, he said, "Bitterness is an unrelenting taskmaster, Johnny—never, ever let it control your life."

Dad didn't comment on the topic much more and simply carried on with his normal end-of-the-day routine.

What seemed like a casual comment at the end of a long day at the car wash became a foundational value implanted deeply into my subconscious mind to be pulled into memory at a time when I desperately needed it. Lorraine's words did just that.

They took me back to an evening when Dad was about sixty—six years before he died. I was having dinner at my parents' place, getting ready to meet a friend at the local billiard hall. As dinner wound down, Dad sat reading his Bible. Suddenly he snapped the book shut, and with great resolve said, "That's it, Agnes, we're going over to your brother's right now. I need to ask for forgiveness."

I knew right away what he was referring to. When I was growing up, there was always an unspoken tension between our family and my mom's brothers, one in particular, and I never really knew what had caused it. We seldom interacted with my uncle or his family, except at special occasions when the whole extended family came together.

I suddenly lost interest in my second helping of dessert. I knew something big was up.

"Why, John?" asked my mother.

"I've lost more than twenty years of my life to bitterness and unforgiveness," he said. I heard the two of them talking in hushed tones, acknowledging the hurt they'd experienced as a result of my uncle's actions.

At one point, my mother straightened up and put her hands on her hips. I heard the concern in her voice. "You'll never get your money back, you know," she said.

"It's not about the money. It's about God and me. It's about the years I've lost to bitterness. It's about the loss of freedom to speak with your family. If I'm going to live what the Bible says, I've got to get things cleared up with your brothers."

I was all ears. What was unfolding was something I had never before seen from my father.

Mom dumped the last of the dishes in the sink while Dad grabbed his keys. As soon as they were out the door, I phoned my friend and cancelled our evening plans. I knew something revolutionary was in the works, and I wasn't about to miss it!

When my parents came home late that night, they were still talking together. I could tell something had changed, because along with the tear-stains on their faces there was a real lightness in their steps despite the lateness of the hour. I didn't know the questions to ask, so I just listened to their conversation. Despite not knowing the details, it was clear that some unforgivable offence which had happened more than twenty years before had finally been cleared up, and the door to that deep hurt and misgiving was now closed.

To this day, I don't know exactly what caused the whole scenario or how it eventually came to be reconciled, but I know that whatever it was, it had held my dad captive for over two decades, and he was glad to be free of it.

And free he was. The Bible had come alive for him in a way that deeply impacted him every day for the rest of his life. With that single sentence about bitterness, spoken at the car wash just a few weeks before he passed away, I was reminded again about that whole situation.

But despite my father's example of how pent-up hurts can so negatively affect the present, my own life didn't reflect any understanding of that. I felt as though every aspect of our lives was unravelling, and it seemed to me like God was continuing to maintain a steadfast silence. He was growing more and more distant all the time.

The more I thought about my situation, the less fair it seemed and the more bitter I became. Pain was constant. Emotions were raw. Behaviour was unpredictable. Relationships were fragile. Nothing made sense. I'd see men out playing with their sons, and I'd resent God's apparent inaction. A friend would close a great business deal, and I'd picture myself just slugging along trying to make ends meet. I knew enough about business that I didn't let myself appear despondent to employees or clients, but once I walked through the front door of my home, my demeanour changed!

I felt like everything about our lives was cascading down into a black abyss. All I'd built in carving out my own identity—determined, perhaps subconsciously, to show the world I was not just my sisters' little brother—was being shattered. Now, with the extra demand on our time and resources required in caring for Byron, I could see there was no way I could simply work harder and faster to take care of things; this was far beyond what I could control.

I'd read somewhere that bitterness is a poison you swallow hoping someone else will die. At that time in my life, there seemed to be some truth in that.

Everything came to a head late one night. As I lay in bed, I could feel the heaviness of the room pressing in on me. The sheets were twisted around me from all my tossing and turning, and every time I turned over it still hurt. I couldn't pull my mind out of its downward spiral as I thought about missed opportunities and looming financial pressures. My heartbeat seemed to speed up with every new scenario that popped unbidden into my head, and I finally had to get up just to maintain a grasp on my sanity.

It must have been about three o'clock in the morning when I stumbled through the dark house into the family room. My big, old leather recliner was there, visible in the dim moonlight coming through the window, and I sat down in it and buried my head in my hands.

"God, it just doesn't make sense!" I cried out. "Nothing makes sense! I'm not hearing anything from You! Our lives are spiralling downward, and the only thing in front of us is a dark hole! It's like everything we are and everything we have is just going down, down, down—all the connections we've made with people in the corporate world, all the opportunities, all the things you've built into me—everything is just dying! I'm trying to find the way to live right, to back Lorraine, but it's all way beyond what I've got in me to do."

I pushed my face harder into my hands.

"Okay, God, I don't have anything else. I guess this is it. I just give in to You." My recent behaviour came to mind, so I carried on in the same breath,

"And forgive me, please, for my anger, my frustration, my bitterness, and my lashing out."

Suddenly, a wave of love swept over me. I felt it wash away all the bitterness and harshness it encountered, and I felt it flow into the deep crevices of my soul. I sobbed my heart out, face buried in my hands, for a long, long time. I cried until there was nothing else in me to cry with, in a mixture of sadness and sorrow, and in release of all my pent-up frustrations. I cried from relief and thankfulness at the love that was cascading over me.

After the sobbing subsided, a deep silence settled over the room. There was a real sacredness about the moment. And in that silence, I clearly heard God speaking to me.

"John, I love you. I never left you. I'll never leave you."

I knew it was true. I had never felt love like that before in my life, and I knew it was Him.

"John, I have plans for your life. But," and there was a pause, "before things get better, they will get worse."

That was all He said. And it was immensely filling. I knew He had said things were going to get worse before they got better, but the certainty that filled me on hearing that God had plans for my life—I can't even describe how comforting that was.

What would I say to Lorraine about what had just happened and what I'd heard?

I headed back to bed with a deep peace filling my whole being.

Resting in the silence, I mulled over what I'd just experienced. I knew something had shifted deep inside of me. I knew we'd be okay, and I knew that although my hopes and dreams still appeared charred and ruined, there was a fresh horizon within sight where things would be different, and where those dreams would again be realized. Still, I was sobered by the understanding that things were going to get worse before they got better.

It took that difficult experience for me to start incorporating my father's words and what he'd learned into my own life. Looking back, I can see that

I'd understood my father's lesson but wasn't able to apply it to my own life until I'd carried the weight of my own unhealed pain and disillusionment. I was glad I'd stored away that experience with my father, because now it was there to draw on when I desperately needed the mental and emotional realignment.

The years continued to be hard and brutal, but it was when I let go of the bitterness that I found the strength to even acknowledge that I wasn't going to give up. Had I not faced my unresolved issues, I would have eventually faced a meltdown of devastating proportions.

It's a luxury to be able to look back and think about things, of course, but I tend to think that the experience of coming to the end of ourselves is of supreme value. We're constantly writing the next chapter of our lives by how we live in the present, with the values we've established. If we haven't hit the wall and come to the end of ourselves, however, we can be writing our future from a shallow, self-focused perspective, basing our hopes merely on what *we* can bring to the equation, and not taking into account the variables over which we truly have no control. We then miss out on the depth of life and influence that God brings to the situation.

When I reached the end of myself, I was left with nothing to fall back on except God Himself. I had been living intentionally, giving back, choosing to pursue the Greater Dream, but helping Lorraine in her role as a full-time caregiver to our brain-injured son had not been part of my equation. Re-entering the world after months spent fighting back from the edge of death had not been in my plan, but in that posture of full release to God and full dependence on Him I was able to let go of the perceived injustices, the un-answerables, and the fear of a future I couldn't see. It was only then that I could rest in the love that Jesus extended to me.

The hospital psychologist's candid comments had been a dose of reality, but it wasn't until I came face to face with my inability to deal with that new reality that I was truly able to understand and appreciate what God had in

His heart for me and for us—and His dream for us superseded the hospital psychologist's most dire warning!

When I finally reached the point of accepting this new reality—by giving up control of my hopes and dreams and letting Jesus take the lead again—I was able to move on. The hard part, of course, was that, right in the middle of my crisis, I could only see the first half of that paradox, the "I'm-no-longer-in-control-of-my-own-destiny" part, the part that had me believing "It's all over."

But that was not to be a one-time lesson. We would face it time and again, in various ways.

More than a year had passed since that fateful day on the highway. The rise in temperatures mirrored the rise in our own levels of optimism, and we decided to slip away from our everyday environment to take a break together as a family. We needed a rest, and this was a good time to take it. Arizona had always been a favourite destination for us, so we packed up and made plans to head south. To keep costs down, we elected to drive, and I have to admit that despite the crash I was really looking forward to getting behind the wheel and spending time together as a family. We'd always loved road trips.

We were all excited. We packed the car, piled in, and headed south. We drove through the night and arrived in Phoenix about noon the next day. Right at the end of the journey, just before we arrived at our hotel, we stopped at a service station to fill the car with gas. Pulling off the highway, the engine started making a funny sound, so before turning it off at the gas pump I opened the hood to check the motor. Everything looked fine, but with the hood up I could hear the solid clunking sound much more clearly, and my heart sank. I knew this wasn't something simple; this had the sound of a major mechanical malfunction. We gassed up and limped off to our hotel, driving slowly and gingerly.

Sure enough, when we nursed the car over to the local Cadillac dealer the following morning to receive their verdict, the problem was big. A main bearing had turned in the engine block, and the engine would require a complete rebuild. Not only that, but with our drive all the way down from Canada we had turned the odometer past the magic number, meaning our warranty had just expired.

What could we do? We left our vehicle to get fixed. Lorraine and I were pretty quiet as we drove back to the hotel in a rental car. So much for keeping costs down! We had so wanted this vacation to be memorable—but not for reasons like this. We did everything we could to still make it an enjoyable time for the boys, but the knowledge that somehow we'd have to pay for a huge repair bill before we headed home really put a damper on things.

Our car was fixed a week later, and we were broke. Nowhere, in any account, did we have the $6,200 needed to pay for the engine rebuild. A couple of years previously, that wouldn't have been a big deal, but now it was overwhelming. With a heavy heart, I returned the rental car and paid for our repair with my American Express card, fully aware that the people at American Express, strangely enough, would want that bill paid in thirty days.

The knowledge that we were still on the hook for the full $6,200 loomed over me the entire way home. Lorraine and I were somewhat apprehensive as to what would happen, but at the same time we were determined to trust God. As we left the city, Brent sat in the back seat with tears running down his cheeks—crying quietly because he didn't want to leave. As we drove, we knew that somehow we'd managed to still have a good family holiday despite the engine trouble.

Back home, the thirty days passed all too quickly. We had nothing extra in our pockets to pay the bill. All we could do that whole month was trust and pray.

On the last Saturday of the month, we drove into town for a family breakfast at a local restaurant. We stopped at the post office on the way back to check our Friday mail. One of the pieces was from the Canadian Wheat Board, which was a bit of a surprise because it wasn't the time of year that they usually sent out their invoices. However, I ripped the envelope open, and what came out was not an invoice, but a cheque! And it was a cheque for $6,800! The accompanying letter explained that a random reassessment of accounts and contributions had turned up the fact that we'd overpaid that amount in wheat board levies several years previously.

Needless to say, we were flabbergasted! To tell the truth, at first we even wondered whether the letter was to be trusted. Nevertheless, first thing Monday morning I took the cheque to the bank and, with great relief, paid off the entire American Express bill—with money to spare. We were awed by our amazing God! He was certainly speaking with thunderous affirmation now!

This whole season of reengagement with life was very different for Lorraine than it was for me. When she was at home, her focus remained on Byron and Brent, giving them the care and attention they needed day to day. I was trying to hold the pieces of our corporate world together.

When we'd finished with dinner and clean-up, when both boys were finally in bed late in the evening, Lorraine and I had time to be together. We talked at length with one another. Even after all the months of her being in the hospital with Byron during the week, we were able to re-establish our connection, and a deeper level of authentic communication became the norm. Our conversations were, at times, pretty tough, because each of us was dealing with completely different sets of challenges and realities. But Lorraine was able to hear my heart, and I hers. At the end of these difficult conversations, we got back to our old practice of holding hands and praying together. That deeper level of communication, and the intimacy that grew from it, became the foundation for us as we continued our journey toward a New Normal.

Joy and laughter slowly replaced the sense of hopelessness and despair. Ever so slowly, we were moving from just coping with life to the place of beginning to dream again. We'd faced a significant tragedy as a family, a tragedy with consequences that would stay with us for the rest of our lives, but we didn't let it become the end of the story. More accurately, God didn't let it become the end of the story, and we were willing enough to respond to His leading in moving us forward.

As we walked forward into the unwritten days of our lives, we found God was able to use the car crash and all its carnage for good—to create instant credibility with individuals who were living in challenging circumstances. We'd always been deeply committed to God and to the church prior to the crash, both as a couple and as a family; now, somehow, people found us all the more believable and easy to trust.

In town one day, I bumped into an old acquaintance, the former administrative assistant to one of my business collaborators. This lady was not a follower of Jesus, and I used to make it a point to speak with her about matters of faith when I dealt with her. Years before our crash, she and her family had suffered a horrific tragedy. She had lost her husband and oldest son in a fire which consumed their house. Now, standing in a bank line together, neither of us had much patience for small talk. After we had greeted each other, she got right to the point:

"So, John, do you still believe?"

I knew she was asking an honest question, so I gave her an honest answer.

"Yes, I do," I said, knowing the pain and history behind her question. "I believe perhaps more quietly, but far more deeply."

I watched as her eyes filled with tears and she quickly left the bank.

That was the extent of our conversation. Before the crash, she'd probably simply tolerated what I expressed about my faith. Now, though, she wanted to know whether my present experience still matched my earlier words. I believe that's where authenticity comes from: when you are tested, what remains?

I found myself starting to wonder what this newfound believability and trust could mean for us. Were there ways Lorraine and I could be making more of a difference in the lives of others?

I know now that we are—all of us—constantly writing "what comes next" in our lives. That late-night session sitting in my old recliner gave me the freedom to set aside what I'd assumed would be the next chapter of my life. It gave me the freedom to pick up the pen and begin writing a new tomorrow for myself and my family, one that included realities I had not thought would be part of our equation.

It was a struggle, but I came through it, and I came through it only after I gave up trying to figure it out for myself. I thought I saw everything fully, and what I thought I saw was overwhelming—but I was only seeing things from my own limited perspective, not from God's bigger view.

Despite how it seemed to me at the time, our tomorrows were still unwritten. The future looked pretty grim after the hospital psychologist's pronouncement, but it took a while for me to see that his perspective wasn't the only choice I had. My willingness to lay down control of the future and accept God's ability to lead me through the darkness of the present was the key to eventually pulling out a fresh sheet of paper and taking the opportunity to write a new tomorrow.

That truth stays with me today. I know there are realities coming for Lorraine and me that we're currently unaware of. I know I've probably made decisions which will have consequences I may not experience or understand until years from now. I know I write things into my life daily which may come back to challenge me later on. Even after our decision to bring Byron home with us, and my wrestling match with God that helped form my resolve, we still had realities and consequences to deal with as a family that didn't show up until years down the road.

But when those realities hit, showing up uninvited with all their messy baggage, I know that giving up is not the answer. I know that even when the dreams seem dead and buried, even when the only possible choice seems to radically undermine my future, there is still an opportunity to hold on to hope.

There is still hope, even when the Hope-Giver is not responding the way I think He should.

Life continued to hammer us, and we certainly weren't getting time off for good behaviour, that's for sure! One of our business interests was a land development company, and we'd broken ground the year before on a subdivision development outside our hometown.

I'd always maintained integrity in my business dealings, and part of that commitment was to deal only with licensed and bonded contractors. I wanted every product or service we offered to be of the highest quality for the price point, even if the buyers weren't aware of the extra care we took.

With this new development, though, I strayed outside my own guidelines and hired a friend to install the underground water services. Rather than insisting on a bonded company, I believed his excuse for not being bonded. In my desire to help him live out his Greater Dream, I signed a contract with him and, in doing so, made a flawed decision that would come back to haunt me and cause immense frustration for a lot of people.

This contractor's job was to lay the water lines that would connect each lot to a regional water supply. The reports I received from him stated that the trenches had been dug alongside the roadways, the waterlines had been laid, and the individual connections had been completed. In my drives around the site, I saw the trenches and the water lines placed into them, and everything looked fine. Elsewhere around the development, construction was moving ahead, foundations were being poured, services were being hooked up, and things were moving along to allow the framers and other subcontractors to work through the winter. As the weather turned cold, many foundations were backfilled and the water service trenches were filled in.

Unbeknownst to me, however, the water services contractor had not connected the main service conduits to the individual lot lines. As the weather turned cold, he simply filled in the trenches and left the junctions unconnected. Neither the building lots nor the homes were actually connected to the regional water supply.

As spring warmed our area, excited homeowners moved into their new residences. But when they turned on their taps to fill their hot water tanks and toilets, nothing happened.

The phone calls started coming into the office. At first everyone thought there was just a minor glitch somewhere in the system, something that could be easily fixed. Soon, though, the realization sank in that there was a major problem. It wasn't until our crews actually traced the lines and dug up the first pipes that they knew the connections hadn't been made.

The contractor, of course, was nowhere to be found. Lorraine and I realized we'd be left holding the bag for this, so we talked and prayed together, searching for a solution that would honour the people who'd bought from us. God remained silent here as well; there were no miraculous changes, it didn't turn out that only one or two houses were affected, and my former "sprinter's faith" didn't seem to be able to solve the situation quickly and easily.

We realized we'd have to deal with this directly and quickly, even while we tried to track down the contractor. We made plans to truck water in daily for the families already living in their new homes. We sent crews in to start digging and fixing the missing connections. The lines all had to be located, dug up, flushed, and properly connected. Some homes already had driveways over the affected areas, others had landscaping, and in other places the roads themselves had to be retrenched so workers could access the water lines. No one was happy.

The lawsuits started. Here I was, home in bed for long periods everyday, completely exhausted after spending the morning in the office, yet trying to think positively. I needed to reserve energy for the rehabilitation I required to get my body functioning, and now my spare time was filled with lawyers. Lorraine had served as controller for a number of our companies, so now she was involved as well, trying to be a support for Byron, trying to be a support for me, and trying to maintain good connection with Brent. It wasn't like her own healing journey was finished, either.

Even though it felt like the "whys" surrounding our life were mounting beyond the answers we were hearing, we decided that integrity was unquestionably the way to walk forward through this minefield. We understood the desperation and anger of the homeowners, and we chose to maintain strong relationships wherever possible by bearing the costs of repairing the damage, even while we countered the lawsuit in court. Being that it was a civil case that would be heard by a judge, we had to bring in another lawyer from out of town who specialized in civil law.

By the time the lawsuit was winding down, the physical repairs to the development had been completed. We no longer had to pay for trucking water, and our legal expenses would soon be capped, but hanging over our heads was the financial uncertainty of the judge's decision. If he sided with the complainants, there was no telling how large a settlement he'd impose.

As had already happened so often during our recovery, we experienced the strength and help of family and friends coming around us to support us in ways we couldn't do for ourselves. Those of our family who lived nearby fasted and prayed for us during the days before the judge's ruling. Lorraine's sister Terri also joined us from her home in Chicago, as did her sister Carol, now at her new placement in Vienna.

Finally, the judge entered the courtroom and, with a swirl, the proceedings were set in motion. He began by outlining the case history and reviewing the documents and statements that had been presented to him over the preceding months. Then he moved to his assessment and decision.

"Mr. Baergen, is your water system repaired now?"

"Yes, Your Honour," I said.

Moments, later we heard the words we hardly dared hope for—"Not guilty! No damages!"

We were elated, to say the least—and deeply grateful. After months of hard work and continued financial drain, we could finally close the door on this unwelcome chapter in our lives. We still carried a full load of challenges—I was still in recovery mode, Bryon still needed us virtually every waking moment, and the whole development fiasco had drained us both emotionally and financially—but we revelled in the moment, knowing our burden would now be a little lighter.

I had a lot of questions for God during this time, but I knew I had to keep moving forward in faith. There was no other way I could face the days. I wasn't depressed or despondent—I simply could not for the life of me understand why all of this was happening.

Yet I still had the sense that underneath everything—deeper even than the faith I was choosing to stand on—there was something else at work, something that hinted at a greater purpose for all the horror we were going through. I had a settled understanding of just knowing God was there, despite the apparent evidence to the contrary. All I could do was trust Him and survive another day on that foundation. On some level, I knew the only thing worth standing on was the belief that God was who He said He was, and that He was trustworthy—even when everything I knew was being shaken to the core. That was part of why I could walk forward one more day without completely losing hope.

And the judge's decision placed another layer of trust on the foundation of my faith.

* * * *

From where John and I find ourselves now—taking stock of what we've been through and how it has shaped our lives from the crash and beyond—we realize we've had a few lessons hammered into us. For instance, when we thought things couldn't possibly get worse, they usually did.

Virtually every time we thought we'd hit rock bottom, something else would rise up out of nowhere and drag us down even further. We learned a powerful lesson from the vantage point of lying on our backs at rock bottom, feeling the ground beneath us give way: our sense of how we're doing on the journey can't be gauged by our circumstances.

When God went silent, we were blindsided! We'd missed the point that God's love for us—His care and concern and affection for us—was not based on how often we prayed or how successfully we'd carried out what we thought He'd asked of us. He didn't love us more because of the quality of our character, or any of the other things we'd subconsciously turned to for gauging how likely God would be to respond to our needs in a way we could see.

We had to be reminded that God's love for us, His unconditional acceptance of us, is based solely on the strength of who *He* is and what *He* has done. It's more about us responding to His lead than it is about Him coming to our rescue.

Another lesson we learned is that no matter what our circumstances, we only see part of the picture. Situations might seem too big to handle. Life can push down so hard that even breathing becomes a chore. But it's still only part of the picture.

When John was still recovering and the subdivision crisis arose, we didn't realize that the "rest of the story," to quote Paul Harvey, was waiting to be written. Because we thought there might be no way out, we initially missed the thread running through every circumstance: our choices in each moment open the door to new possibilities in the next, and our choices there lead to even further possibilities in the *next* moment.

John's choice to continue believing "no matter what" set the tone for his next set of possibilities. It was the same for me when I chose to persist in my faith, even though Byron wasn't miraculously healed. Had either of us chosen differently, we probably wouldn't have made it out of our circumstances successfully—but we didn't know that at the time.

Everything that followed was still unwritten. It was our responses and choices moment by moment and day by day that turned the unwritten into the written as it stands today.

Many people I've talked with remember having dreams at various points in their lives regarding what they'd like to do or accomplish in their lifetimes. Perhaps there were businesses they wanted to start, or life purposes they felt called to. For John and me, the dreams weren't necessarily that clearly articulated; we just had a vague longing for something more, something else we were made for. But we knew we had deeper dreams beyond what we'd experienced.

Life can be pretty adept at killing those deeper dreams, or at least beating them down so they never resurface. Sometimes the careless words of a schoolteacher destroy a student's aspirations. Or a parent's impatience douses the spark of a child's desire. I know people who've managed to keep their dreams alive into adulthood, only to have a cheating spouse disillusion them, or to have a harsh working environment slowly pass on its toxins and wear the dream away. The media loves to tell stories about admired business people or religious leaders getting caught cheating the system or hurting others, and it doesn't take many stories like that to slowly burn away one's sense of hope in ever living out the Greater Dream.

For John and me, it was the car crash that seemed to close off any hope of achieving our Greater Dream. I've lived enough to know that sometimes day-to-day life, with its pressures and demands, can slowly asphyxiate the spark of joy we once felt, leaving instead a dull ache that follows us to bed and whispers to our inner ear, as we lay our head down on the pillow, that we're wasting our lives and there's no point to anything.

But I also know it doesn't have to be that way.

Sitting here today—pondering all that we've been through—I know that John and I have come to believe that the spark can still be fanned into flame. We've seen through the lie that says there's no way out. We've come to know that no matter what our circumstances may be telling us today, and no matter how we came to be in those circumstances, tomorrow, next week, and the rest of our lives can still become the best and most fulfilling days of our lives, because their path is still to be set: the days to come are still unwritten.

That's what I see today. But the year after the crash, when physical and financial recovery consumed every waking moment of our lives, I couldn't see much of that at all. The intervening years were still unwritten at that point. The strongest thing I could do for myself back then was to keep picking up my pen and writing "I stand on Your Word" in the margin of my Bible whenever I came across a truth that seemed so far removed from the reality of my family's life.

In making that choice, to believe despite the circumstances, I discovered that I could get up each morning and pull out my Bible yet again. I could care for Byron without completely giving in to despair that nothing would change for him.

Musings

CHAPTER 8

HOPE GLIMMERS

A seed germinates when no one is watching.

That's how hope first started to appear for us. We'd come to accept, for the most part, the New Normal our lives were heading toward, and were slowly coming back to an even keel. We were learning how to care for Byron. We were starting to rebuild our businesses so we could refill the financial hole instead of making it deeper. Even if our heads were not quite yet above water, we could at least see the surface.

Gradually our focus shifted to re-engaging as a family. For Brent and me, recovery started almost within hours of the crash, and we relied upon family and friends right from the start. Both Byron and John, however, remained in survival mode for weeks, time in which we all wondered whether or not they would even live. Eventually they, too, shifted out of survival into recovery, and it was in that shift that we all relied so heavily upon the love and care of family and friends.

For Byron, returning to school meant attending a school for the challenged. That whole process was excruciatingly difficult. It's hard for me to even find the words to describe the pain involved in coming to terms with it. Even though Byron could not express much outwardly, I was sure he understood internally the vast contrast for him in his new situation.

Six weeks after Byron finally returned home from the hospital, it was time for the school Christmas program, and he was asked to place an ornament on the tree as part of the pageant. An aide pushed his wheelchair across the platform to the tree, and Byron hung his ornament on a low-hanging branch. As his chair was wheeled back across the stage, a tear ran down his cheek, and I could feel my heart breaking for him. It was impossible not to recall our church's Christmas program only twelve months earlier, when Byron had been the narrator. We were crushed, but there was nothing we could do other than accept life's present circumstances and continue to move forward.

At about the same time, Byron showed us through humour that he was adjusting to his New Normal. At the end of each school day, staff helped students get on their outside clothes and then pushed their wheelchairs up against the wall in the hallway to wait for the bus. On one occasion, Byron noticed he'd been placed near the fire alarm, so he surreptitiously raised his arm above his head, pulled the alarm, and set the bell clanging. Needless to say, knowing the alarm was coming from a school made for a swift response from the fire crews in the area, and fire trucks started arriving quickly. As firemen ran into the school hallway, Byron started laughing with a tone of voice that was clearly expressing: "See? I am much smarter than you think I am!"

It was his way of dealing with frustration, of course, but it proved he knew more and was capable of more than anyone realized. Our New Normal meant we had to accept Byron's emerging limitations, but to this day it also means we must acknowledge Byron as a person who is more resilient and profound than what his outward appearance would suggest. Byron always surprises people who spend time with him. The depth of person locked into that body is amazing, and we've yet to discover the key that will set him free.

Although I was not aware of the long-term picture back then, the struggle of that season marked a turning point in my journey. It was as though an internal switch had been thrown deep inside me. Very slowly, almost imperceptibly at first, the journey was now turning from a downward slide into an uphill motion, and each step I took was now leading me forward into tomorrow. God had been achingly silent, or so it seemed, and He had apparently not acted on Byron's behalf as we'd envisioned, despite our most fervent prayers. But here, at rock bottom, I was finding that He was still my Rock. He was the Rock I could still stand on and even sink my roots into.

I was learning how to write the next pages of my unwritten future.

As we had now moved well into the second year post-accident, it became clear that the cold climate in our home region was taking its toll on our recovering bodies. We started talking about moving somewhere warmer, which brought excitement but also a sense of loss. Moving would not only mean giving up the comfort of our present livelihood, but also leaving the extended family and friends who'd become such a huge part of our lives. It also meant leaving a church family that had stood alongside us during the darkest days of our lives, and heading to a place where we had no relationships. Given how traumatic the previous two years had been, we were looking forward to a fresh start.

It was clear God was now leading us somewhere, and the plan began to unfold. Though we couldn't initially see where we'd go and how we'd get there, we moved forward, expecting God to make the way clear.

At first we thought we might go to Arizona. We'd always enjoyed our stays there, and the climate was perfect for us. But the more we looked into all that would be required for us to live there rather than just visit, the more we realized it just wouldn't be realistic to make Scottsdale our new home.

So, with a better understanding of where we weren't going but without a clear picture of where we *would* end up, we packed everything and took the long drive out to western Canada. We stopped for a while in Vancouver, and then ended up choosing a city in the Okanagan Valley. About two years after our crash, we closed down our interests back home and settled our family into this warm and pleasant location, ready and eager to move forward into whatever the future held for us.

Leaving our hometown and community of relationships meant there were a lot of goodbyes to be said. In the final week before we moved, we met with our pastor Del and his wife. Del's silent support of us during our earliest times of recovery had been so meaningful that we wanted to connect one last time before heading out.

"I wonder sometimes," said Del, "if someday we'll be in ministry together." It was an off-handed comment made in the middle of a long conversation, but it stuck with both John and me. I found myself pondering it many times as we packed our lives into boxes and said goodbye to the community that had been so central to us for so many years.

After our move, John and I continued the process of reviewing our goals. Just a few weeks after settling into our new place, we found there was a significant shift in the way we saw things. Del's comment from weeks before kept rising to the surface, and we both wondered what that meant for our future. We started speculating about investing our lives in full-time ministry of some sort, like pastoring in a church. As we continued dreaming and looking ahead, moving toward full-time ministry became one of our five-year goals. Once it was down on paper and part of the process, it wasn't long until we made it one of our three-year goals.

Glimpses of fresh life started to permeate our day-to-day existence. The choices we'd made along the way, the aspects of choosing to believe even when the evidence caused us to doubt, left us with a foundation we could stand on confidently. I had no idea whether we'd ever get to the place where we could live out the Greater Dream, but the person I was becoming seemed right. I could sense God shaping me into a person who could truly live out the purpose for which He had created me.

John, too, was undergoing significant change, even as his body continued its physical healing. He will always have a driven personality, because that's who he is, but I could clearly see that John was allowing God and the circumstances of life to shape that drive into a true inner strength. As he tackled the parallel challenges of rebuilding both physically and financially, I could tell he was relaxing more and more, trusting God to do the rebuilding along with him. I knew that all the strength he was used to was now being reconstructed in ways that would allow him to live out the deeper purposes for which he had been created.

By the time we established ourselves in the Okanagan Valley, we were feeling the desire to reach outside ourselves and start impacting others in the same way we had been influenced. We were still very much in the adjustment phase, of course, learning especially how Byron's new level of abilities would shape the way we functioned as a family. But we believed, deep inside, that God had a purpose for us that was far greater than what we'd seen so far.

An investment consultant called me one day with a concern about a woman who'd just left his office. She was single, pregnant, and very alone. Would I meet with her? Days later, the young woman and I were sitting across from each other, and I heard her heartrending story firsthand.

The two of us began to develop a friendship, and soon this young woman also joined a discussion group where she wrestled through the issues of faith. Although she'd spent time in church before, faith had always been an abstract notion that she couldn't apply to the realities of her life. In this community of people who loved her and cared about her, faith now began to make sense, and she longed for a real relationship with Jesus. Months later, around our dining room table, she made a decision that completely changed the trajectory of her life, moving beyond the abstract and entering into a tangible faith relationship with God.

We've been delighted to see the way this young woman's life has changed as a result of her commitment. We even had the honour of hosting her wedding in our yard and participating in the ceremony. She now works in a church, and together with her new husband she is leading her family toward a Christ-centred life.

Part of becoming established in our new city meant finding a way to earn a living. We took advantage of our previous business experience and started a human resources firm that helped companies find the people they needed.

We also provided practical career support for men and women making career changes. We enjoyed meeting and getting to know our clients, and the network of connections which grew out of this business was quite amazing. People who are in career transition, especially when that transition has been foisted upon them, are often at a very vulnerable place in their lives. We have story after story of the way God was able to step into various situations and bring hope and career direction far beyond our experience or wisdom.

We charged an hourly rate to help clients assess their skillsets and compare them to the type of work they wanted to pursue. But often we'd stop the clock to help people in more personal ways. On countless occasions, John would stop by my office and say: "Hey, Lorraine, Danny and I are going for lunch." When that happened, I'd know that, once again, he was helping a client wrestle with the deeper issues of life. I knew they'd engage in the kinds of conversations John always wished he could have had with his friend Lionel all those years before.

It wasn't like we'd received a vision from heaven regarding starting the HR company, but as time went on we saw the way God was able to use the connections that developed. We knew that we were definitely in business with a far deeper purpose than simply providing career direction.

We met one gentleman, Franco, who was originally trained as a chef in Europe, but who'd been working in a Canadian restaurant for several years. Dissatisfied with greasing cookie sheets, Franco hoped to branch into something new.

We took him through the initial stages of interaction and assessment, and John then spent time with him individually. The two of them carefully reviewed Franco's skill-assessment portfolio, identifying his current frustrations and unique strengths. At the end of it all, John challenged Franco to step out of his comfort zone and start his own restaurant—to move forward with confidence, using the unique specialities he had which would set him apart as a chef.

We both enjoyed watching as Franco worked out a lease with the city on a heritage building where he could establish his own restaurant. One of the characteristics that set his restaurant apart and lent it a first-rate reputation in the city was the ice sculptures he had on display. His gratitude for how John challenged him and helped lead him to his ideal career kept Franco connected to us in friendship for many years.

Another connection developed with a couple who'd moved into the city. Melvin was a power engineer and Donna was in retail clothing sales and marketing. They were contemplating an overseas work assignment. As we spent time together with these two, we sensed in them a growing interest in spiritual matters. They joined a group who met at our house to discuss faith issues, and soon made the critical decision of inviting Jesus to direct their lives. Faith became central to their life journeys from that point on.

Again, our vision of hosting barbecues and meals with a purpose beyond food found its way to the surface, and when our old friend Dr. Terry Winter was able to come and speak at one of these events, we knew we were in the right place. Our affirmation was to see the ways God's network could constantly pull people together: on more than one occasion, we were able to display eye-catching ice sculptures courtesy of our friend Franco, the European chef.

Musings

CHAPTER 9

ROOTS DEEPEN

The spruce trees stood as tall sentries, majestic and silent in their guard along the creek bank. It was quite a sight, with the limbs moving quietly in the slight breeze and the burbling creek adding its peaceful song. But we knew six or seven of the trees would have to be moved to allow us to build. Building our home, enjoying the warmer climate, knowing that God had a greater plan in our lives... combined, these brought a hint of hope that we were just beginning to recognize.

Lorraine was at home with the boys, and I was at the building site with the crew, trying to decide what should be done about these trees. What happened next remains with me to this day as a vivid illustration of what God was up to in our lives.

We'd tried to dig under the roots to facilitate easier removal, but the trees were so large and had such deep and complex root systems that the builder's large front-end loader couldn't do the job. The local Caterpillar dealer happened to have a demo unit of a huge new Cat loader/excavator, so when the builder called him, looking for advice, the dealer volunteered to bring it to the site and try his hand at removing the trees.

It was impressive, I thought, watching this machine take over where the front-end loader had left off. Even though the roots spread out at least forty feet around the base of each tree, the Cat was able to dig down the necessary five to seven feet around the whole system to get under the bulk of the roots. The builder then backed his dump truck up to the trunk of each tree and slowly pushed it over, disengaging the roots from the soil. The loader easily scooped under the roots and lifted the tree from its hole.

Finally, it was four o'clock and we were down to the last tree. While we were impressed with this new Cat, all of us were ready to be done with the whole tree removal process. The job had taken far longer than we had expected, due to the strength and depth of each tree's roots, and we were all looking forward to the weekend. The Cat did its digging, and the truck backed up to the tree to begin pushing it off its base. The tree started leaning; all of a sudden, there was a crescendoing *swooshing* sound, and the tree slammed over to the ground, taking with it all the power lines in the immediate vicinity.

While the other six trees had grown strong and stubborn roots, the seventh had survived with shallow roots. While the other trees took every bit of machine strength and know-how just to get them to lean over, this tree literally caved in under pressure and even, as it collapsed, took out everything else around it. It looked the same as the others, giving the appearance of standing strong and tall, but there was nothing below the surface to stabilize it when the Cat came calling.

Not surprisingly, neither the utility company nor our new neighbours were happy with us—we'd taken out power to the whole area late on a Friday afternoon.

All these years later, those root systems stand out in my mind. Strong and deep root systems take time to grow; they push deeper and wider in search of water for sustenance and stability. Perhaps the last tree had too easily found everything it needed in its place along the creek bank, because the resulting root system was too weak to withstand anything other than normal circumstances. Had we removed the trees around it and left that one standing, it would've been only a matter of time until a strong wind pushed it over. The pressure we'd exerted with our heavy equipment only revealed the weakness already there.

It wasn't until much later that I realized how clearly that episode illustrated what we were going through as individuals and as a family. We knew we were making progress, but the process seemed painstaking, and sometimes unbearably slow. For the most part we'd come to terms with our reality, although we still expected Byron to receive a miracle, but the anticipated climb back from devastation to normality just did not seem to be happening as quickly as we had hoped. I can see now that our roots were growing—slowly but surely.

Lorraine and I believe we were being given a choice. We could either give up, or we could push through those circumstances by standing firm on our conviction that God was in control of our lives. Day by day, we were faced with the choice of either believing everything was hopeless, that life was over, or believing that God was ultimately still in control despite everything we saw around us. It was not an easy walk. Day by day, each choice wrote out a new path for the next day, and after a while we were able to find each day's path with a bit more clarity and a little less struggle.

It was a stretch, though, and there were more than a few days when I gave up and just sat down, mentally, in my discouragement. On those days, I don't know if outwardly I seemed that much different to those around me, and usually I was back on track by the next morning, but at times this process of establishing deeper roots by living through hard and unchanging circumstances really took me off centre.

Lorraine and I have seen the same process at work in others. It's easy to see when someone has chosen to give up rather than press on. We recently heard the story of a friend named Delores who'd been hired to work the front desk at a local company. It became clear early on that Delores was in over her head. Management had asked her to train others in effective customer service, but as time went on, everyone around her could see this was new territory for her—and she wasn't doing well in coping with the expanded mandate. Rather than fire her, though, management offered to pair her with a leadership coach for a year. Unable to accept her change in status, however, Delores resigned rather than embrace the gift being given to her. She'd come to the end of her experience, but rather than explore new horizons she opted out and returned to more familiar territory.

We've seen the same thing in the lives of men and women serving as leaders in churches across the country. In essence, they have three or four years' of work experience, and they repeat that same experience over and over, moving on to a new location rather than working through hard realities.

I'm sure it's the same in business, when a new executive arrives and workers experience the warm glow of a new person with fresh ideas. After two or three years, though, when the novelty wears off and difficulties begin to surface, it's easy for that executive to conclude that things are just not working out, and that it's time to step down and pursue a new position. In the process, each of these individuals circumvent the Greater Dream and settle for something less.

Our roots can only grow deep to the level of challenge we're willing to face. That tall and majestic spruce stopped sending its roots deeper once it reached a supply of water—and when push literally came to shove, there was no depth to anchor it.

While good in theory, this philosophical reflection was far from clear when we were in the midst of our crisis. When we were being given the opportunity to stretch our roots that much deeper, it did not feel majestic! It felt painful, and long, and dry, and hard—each day we simply hung on, trying to make it through.

But that long, hard dryness is what it takes to make the tree force its roots deeper, and it took the same thing to force us to push deeper into our faith. Before the wreck, business was good, prayers were answered, and opportunities seemed endless. After the crash, we were dealing with physical healing, severe financial challenges, and all the extended care, emotional strain, and family-life issues of Byron's new reality. It felt like God was remaining silent through the whole thing—which amplified the hardness and dryness.

I suppose I could have said, "That's it! I quit!" and just given up. I suppose I could have given up being a husband to Lorraine, or a dad to Byron and Brent, or trying to rebuild our business interests, but I wasn't willing to see any of those as options. And as for my own healing, quitting wasn't even a possibility. I couldn't just say, "That's enough, no more pain!"—it just doesn't work that way.

So I kept going, much like Lorraine with her choice to stand on God's Word no matter what our circumstances were saying. We hung on, and the hardness and dryness kept going, too, doing its work of pushing our roots deeper and deeper.

Every once in a while something would happen, even something relatively small, which would give us a bit of encouragement and cause to believe that maybe our family's downward trajectory was starting to flatten out, or even point upwards.

It was becoming clear that Byron wasn't going to be bedridden, so we had to plan for his future and come to grips with the impact that would have on us. For instance, an agonizing change for me was letting go of my dream that Bryon and Brent would someday join me in the family businesses. I had always envisioned a future where both boys would stand shoulder to shoulder with me, but it was becoming increasingly clear that Byron would never be able to fulfill such a role, short of a miracle from God, and it was a slow burn for me to accept that.

One day, Byron started taking his first faltering steps on the driveway, holding on to the handholds of his wheelchair and gingerly moving himself forward under his own power. One step after another, concentrating hard to pick up one foot and then the other as high as he could, shifting his weight from side to side so he could get some forward momentum happening—that was a good day!

Still, it took me a long time before I was willing to take Byron to church. For the longest time, I wasn't prepared to handle the stares I knew Byron would receive. I hated the thought of our little boy being viewed as a public spectacle. Lorraine didn't seem to have the same issues, and I knew I was wrestling with my own internal acceptance of something over which I had no control. It was easier for me to just slip off to church with Lorraine and Brent.

Eventually, though, I came to terms with my own issues, and we started bringing Byron with us on Sundays. It was a new step for us, and it was difficult. We reacted strongly when we saw people actually turn their chairs for a better look, although we knew that for the most part those looks came out of a sincere sense of pain for us. We knew these people were our friends, but it was still hard. We steadfastly stayed the course. I knew attending church as a family, a piece of our old normal, was a necessary hurdle to overcome in our progress toward a New Normal.

Every once in a while, I'd have a moment or two of losing my centeredness, where reality would hit me afresh and the walls of doubt would rush in toward me again, even if just briefly. I found there were certain things we had espoused with great conviction before the crash that now had huge question marks around them. In those brief moments, I would dejectedly wonder if anything was ever going to change—could anything good ever come of this mess?

*   *   *   *

Though John and I were on parallel paths, we were certainly walking our own journeys. We each had to deal with our own internal pain. I couldn't fully understand John's struggles, nor could he empathize with mine. We felt alone as individuals, as a couple, and as a family—we didn't know anyone who'd ever walked this journey and who could therefore truly understand what we were going through.

Brent was also walking his own journey. But with all our concern about Byron's future, we missed the impact this had on Brent. He got lost in the shuffle. His ability to handle the world around him seemed strong, so we believed he was okay. However, our intentional focus on Byron unwittingly fertilized those seeds of abandonment planted earlier in Brent. It wasn't until years later that we came to understand how deeply abandoned he felt, and how injurious it had been for him during those years. It impacted him long into the future.

While people continually invested into Byron's life, our sweet son Brent stood by wondering where he fit in. When people observed our family, Byron was seen as dealing with the most significant challenges and changes, John was still noticeably on a physical recovery road, and I had a lot to deal with in terms of coordinating Byron's care. Brent was seen, often, as being the growing boy who had recovered from his injuries and was doing well back in normal life. Yet there was a struggle going on inside him; he didn't talk about it, but every once in a while I would notice it popping out in his actions or conversation.

I don't think he could express the extent of the pain he felt. Before the crash, Brent had looked up to Byron as his hero. Those roles had been reversed; it was now older-brother Byron who wanted to be wherever younger-brother Brent was. Brent came to accept this, but his friends couldn't, and so they seldom came to the house to play. As a result, part of Brent's New Normal was loneliness—and with John and me at full capacity elsewhere, we could not fully enter his world.

Brent came up with his own ways and means of dealing with that. He was part of a children's choir at our church, and was looking forward to his part in an upcoming concert. The choir director invited Byron to join the choir and participate in the concert as well. Byron's contribution to the concert was minimal; he mainly sat in his chair as part the group, curled over at the waist. Brent sang his heart out, joyfully singing all the songs the ensemble had learned for the concert.

As we left the church, a number of people stopped by our family group to speak with Byron and tell him how well he'd done. It wasn't until I tucked Brent into bed that he gave voice to the thoughts he must have been stewing about since the concert.

"Why did the people say Byron did so well?" he asked. "Didn't I do well, too?"

My heart sank. I hadn't realized the extent to which Brent had been noticing the focus on Byron.

"Oh, Brent, you did really well, and I'm sure people noticed that. But with Byron's disability, with all the challenges he faces, it makes people want to do something to help him. Sometimes they think the only thing they can do is say kind and encouraging words to him."

I searched Brent's face to see if he understood or believed what I was saying. He appeared okay with everything, and we chatted about it a bit more before I kissed him goodnight.

Looking back these twenty-some years later, I see there were many times like this when Brent's heart broke a little more, and then a little more. Slowly but surely, Brent's little heart was closed down further through the painful realities which now defined his life. His feelings of abandonment were complicated by the change in Byron, the change in our family dynamics, and even the change in people's expectations of him. Each of these alone would cause confusion and pain, but together they were overwhelming for a boy his age.

We were definitely charting new territory. Each day, we decided how to write the next segment of our unwritten story. As every day passed, we stood on the foundation of the previous choices we'd made. I'm convinced that our earlier commitment to pray together daily kept our marriage from shattering, as the hospital psychologist had predicted it would. We were alone, yes, but we remained strong in our conviction that God still had plans for us—that it wasn't too late for the Greater Dream.

Looking back, I see the merit in our misery. Hanging on during those trying times meant writing the next lines of our unwritten life story one word at a time, but it also meant we were growing stronger and more stable one root at a time. It wasn't about seeing the ultimate dream being realized instantly; it was about trusting that someday we'd look back and know that God was forming us to live lives of fullness, freedom, and purpose.

It was January again. Every once in a while, I would see John standing at the living room window, looking out on the landscape and sighing to himself. If he spotted me, he'd often wonder out loud whether this was all there was to life, or comment about wanting his life to count for something more.

At first, his frame of mind would frustrate me. *Can't we ever be satisfied?* I'd ask myself as I left the room to help Byron with something or other. I knew our lives already counted for something; we were parents to two special young men, and we were continuing to look for ways to give back to the community even as we got back on our feet. I, too, had noticed how we seemed more credible to people after our crash, and how our sphere of influence was expanding.

We decided to let ourselves dream big again. We brought paper and pens to our times together, laying out what we wanted our five-year goals to be. After that, we got bolder, moving our sight closer to where we were in the present, and we laid out some three-year goals. We weren't outlandish; we focused on milestones we knew we already wanted for our family and businesses—but just the fact that we were looking forward again, rather than being stuck in the moment, was in itself encouraging and strengthening.

Even though John and I have each had very significant encounters with God over the years, sometimes I think our tendency to always want to push on into the Greater Dream may originally have found its roots in the prayers of our parents. My mom and dad both had a great desire for the things of God. Right after John and I were first married, they attended a conference which impacted them deeply. They learned spiritual truths and principles for living the Christian life at a level deeper than they'd ever experienced as committed church leaders. They learned about living a life that displayed power and strength beyond the ordinary because it found its source of strength outside of itself—namely, in Jesus. And they learned a lot more about introducing people to Jesus.

This conference had such a strong impact on them that Dad and Mom turned their sights on us. They did everything they could to convince us to go. And we did. Very likely, that experience played a large role in our lifelong desire to influence others. We learned truths that resonated with the passion deep in our hearts.

John's experience at the conference was more dramatic than mine. At one point, those of us attending the conference were expected to put the skills and principles we were learning into practice. We were joined with another couple, more senior and experienced than we were, to pay a visit to people in the community. The idea was to use an articulate, well-planned approach to introduce people to the person of Jesus by precisely and clearly communicating the difference He had made in our lives. We were simply to tell our story.

When it came time to head out on our afternoon of skills practice, John was nowhere to be found. A quick search, however, turned him up in the bathroom, trying to keep out of sight so he would hopefully miss the afternoon's activities.

But he joined us, and we both learned a great deal through our encounters with normal, everyday people in the community. We learned that people actually do want to discuss the deeper aspects of life, that they want answers to their questions, and that they really do respond to authentic stories of life change. The majority of people are open to God encounters, we discovered, when those experiences are presented in genuine and non-threatening ways.

The truths we learned that week have stayed with us through the various seasons of our lives. That conference took place early in our marriage, so those shared experiences were written into our foundations, both as individuals and as a couple. They fuelled the fire for living the Greater Dream, for carrying out that which God set before us right from the beginning. If our holy discontent wasn't born in that setting, it certainly was stirred up and brought to life there, and from that point forward we've never been content to settle for less than God's best dream for us.

We had the assurance that we were still on track with living the Greater Dream. That was our overarching theme. Had we stayed with the safety of what we'd already established, we would have been settling for the lesser dream.

Globally, the financial situation was still tenuous, but our little HR company was holding its own, and even expanding. The operation was settling into a comfortable groove, and John had just finalized a deal to acquire one of our key local competitors—a temporary placement agency—when suddenly one of our longer-term goals became an immediate possibility, if we were open and ready for it.

An invitation had come from a large church located near the city where John and Byron had spent so much time in hospital. Would John be interested in being a candidate for the role of executive pastor?

The invitation threw us into a bit of a quandary, albeit a good one. This was definitely one of our goals, but the fact that the opportunity had come now, rather than three years down the road as we had set the goal for, forced us to look at whether we were comfortable stepping off our own map and being willing to jump through doors God was opening—if, in fact, He was opening them!

The church was pastored by our old friend Del. That comment from years before about working together came back to mind. Was this the time we'd see the fruition of that?

For John, it wasn't as easy a decision, although he was very intrigued. The role of executive pastor was new at this church, so John would be building it from the ground up. That was completely in line with what he liked to do, and the fact that we'd be serving with Del was another strong pull.

At the same time, there was our HR business to think about. It was established now and continuing to grow. The acquisition of the competing HR company meant there were challenges and opportunities right at home that John could sink his teeth into, so it wasn't like he was lacking something to do. And with the economic climate being what it was, would we be able to sell the business if we accepted the pastoring role? For that matter, would our house sell? Furthermore, the church didn't allow immediate family members to serve together in paid staff positions. John and I had always worked together, and we were committed to moving forward as a team.

"That's not acceptable, Lorraine," John said to me as we were pondering our choices. "With all we've been through, we've come to know so clearly that we are made to serve God together. I don't want to be found in a place where you are not living out God's greater purpose and plan for your life."

We decided we wouldn't even go as candidates unless the church leaders assured us we'd both be hired.

Still, the longer we prayed about it and the more we talked about it, the more we became sure that God was in the whole thing. So, taking the words from *The Message* translation of the Bible seriously—"...*when two of you get together on anything at all on earth and make a prayer of it, my Father in heaven goes into action*" (Matthew 18:19)—we agreed together that we wanted to take the next step toward this opportunity. We prayed, and we started working through what seemed to be obstacles or challenges.

John went into negotiations with the church's board, and the board agreed to put aside their policy on nepotism and hire both of us. Out of nowhere, it seemed, we received a call from a distant acquaintance asking if the business was for sale. Conversation continued, negotiations began, and the sale was completed before we made any attempts to sell through conventional means. There was no doubt in our minds that God had set the ball in motion. Our house sold, too, even in a depressed real estate market.

The one thing which remained, something we decided we would simply have to live with, was the aspect of returning to a colder climate. We'd chosen our current city because the weather was more conducive to our family's physical healing. Now we'd be heading back to a place where the weather could again become a problem. But we had the assurance that God was leading us forward, and we hoped that, with the years of healing and restoration we'd already enjoyed, the impact of the colder climate would not be as severe as it had been previously.

Now, as things kicked into gear, we could see that the New Normal was definitely not an unchanging destination.

Musings

CHAPTER 10

NORMAL'S OVER

"Hey, Baergen—is that really you?"

I whirled around, as much as whirling was possible on crutches, trying to recognize the voice. This was a number of years ago, and I was in between flights at the Minneapolis airport, on my way home from a conference in Chicago. I'd had further corrective surgery not long before my trip, and was back on crutches.

I couldn't quite pick out where the voice had come from.

"Baergen, over here!"

I turned again and saw a middle-aged man quickly making his way over to where I was standing. He looked familiar, but it took a few moments for me to place him. Ahhh, now I had it! He owned the Ford dealership back in our original hometown.

"Jim!" I called out. "It's good to see you!"

"I thought that was you!" Jim said as he came over. "You old son of a so-and-so… it's been years! I couldn't believe it when I saw you making your way down the concourse on those crutches. You know what? Remember that last barbeque at your house, when the fellow from NATO spoke?"

Jim was referring to the last barbecue we'd hosted before moving west.

"I can hardly believe it," he continued. "I was actually thinking about that today. Your friend from NATO asked each of us, 'Which wall is your ladder up against?' And then I see you here in this airport in Minneapolis. This is amazing!"

Nimrod McNair, my friend from NATO, had challenged us to consider how the choices we make add up and grow one step on top of the other, much like a ladder. Sometimes we get so focused on building our lives that we don't realize we're leaning our ladder against the wrong wall. Then, when we get to the top and peer over, on that final day of our life, we suddenly see we're not in a place we want to be.

I knew this was not a chance encounter with Jim. Even the fact that I was on crutches made it easier for him to recognize me. That's how he would have remembered me from our last meeting.

We spent the next hour catching up. We'd known each other before the barbecue, which is why Lorraine and I had invited him to attend. After the event, we met again to talk further about where he was at in life. But with our move and all, we simply lost contact. Now, all these years later, he was still thinking about that conversation and asking himself which wall his ladder was leaning against. God had seen fit to arrange a meeting for us a thousand miles away from where either of us lived. It blew me away.

This type of encounter was not uncommon. Time after time, we saw how our story resonated with people, and how the journey we walked affected the ways in which others walked theirs.

When we first became aware of this, we asked many questions. If God wants to use our story to help others, how then do we live the rest of our lives? Is there a way to leverage that for the greatest Kingdom impact? How do we stay centred in Jesus, so we never lose sight of the bigger picture?

This insight had already begun to take shape by the time we accepted the invitation to join the church. I was executive pastor, and Lorraine was leading women's ministries; both roles were new to the church, and we were crafting them as we moved forward. Deep inside, we wondered if our daily post-crash challenges would limit our effectiveness at the church. But rather than hindering our professional lives, we found that the everyday timbre of our lives, the feet-on-the-earth reality of living with a son who was suffering the impact of brain injury and needing hands-on care, enabled us to quickly move from peripheral issues to those of the heart. More often than not, our situation opened doors deep into the lives of the people we served.

We learned how God takes difficult situations, those we expect will destroy our chance for the Greater Dream, and arranges them so they actually strengthen us and move us forward. At the same time, we learned that we had to stop looking inward all the time, letting go of the "rights" we still held so tightly, so God could fuel the passion for our Greater Dream of making a meaningful difference in the lives of others. We had to give Him permission to do that. Once we did, our crash and its resulting lifelong challenges became a bridge that opened up new relational territory.

We'd seen that clearly when we first moved out west, just two years after the car wreck. With Byron still in a wheelchair, and us struggling to adapt, it was the young adults who took note of us and seemed to connect with the raw reality of who we were. Our home became the gathering place for spiritual conversations with those new friends. Now, at this new church, we saw that scenario playing out again. All we had to offer was brokenness and an authentic connection with people—and those we served responded to that quickly and with trust.

There was a time when a family from another province heard about our story and drove out to meet us. Their own story was one of complete tragedy, and our hearts broke when we heard their journey: they had five children, all boys. The oldest of the sons had decided to take his younger brothers on a ski trip as a Christmas gift. Full of excitement, and with the call of brotherly adventure ringing in their ears, the boys had all piled into one of the family vehicles and headed off, only to be involved in a crash which killed all four of the younger brothers and left the older brother brain-injured.

After hearing our story, and knowing our faith in Jesus, this family felt they'd found someone who could truly empathize with them. The devastation and loss they'd suffered was beyond our comprehension, but it confirmed that we wanted to invest our lives into people who had lost hope for the restoration of their Greater Dream.

Lorraine and I never found we had to work too hard at bringing the deeper things of life into the present moment. Our dependency upon God kept us mindful of His role in our daily lives, and that consciousness spilled over into regular group conversations about spiritual matters. God was not something or someone we merely tacked onto our busy North American lives. He was real, and living at the core of our beings. His strength alone enabled us to survive and move forward day by day. People seemed to appreciate that, and we had strong and consistent connections with those around us who wanted to engage in deeper spiritual dialogue.

On the financial front, the long legal battle we had initiated years earlier developed into a too-long battle. Our issue was not the money, per se, but what the money could do for Byron. The initial stages of dealing with his brain injury were the most critical, and without adequate financial resources his rehabilitation would be compromised. Time was critical; the sooner Byron got the help he needed, the better he would respond. Medical personnel were clear in their assessment of Byron's need—the first two years of post-head injury rehabilitation would result in the greatest progress. We'd already passed that milestone, and still nothing was happening with our case.

Lorraine's sister gave us the name of a renowned accident insurance attorney, one recognized for getting swift and successful closure in cases like ours. We agonized over our decision; after all, our current lawyer had become a close friend. We knew we'd risk our friendship if we changed lawyers, but with things as they were, we were risking Byron's future. We decided to change firms. And it was a good choice—the case was finalized relatively quickly from that point.

We even paid our first lawyer from the settlement, hoping to preserve something of our connection. Unfortunately, though, he resented our switch, and we lost contact with him. We were saddened by that. Post-crash, we'd learned to value the people in our lives, and it was disheartening to lose the friendship of someone we'd come to value.

Years later, we needed a lawyer to process some simple documents. Lorraine suggested that I approach the lawyer who had first taken our insurance case, as he lived and worked in the community we'd moved to. She figured it would give us an opportunity to reconnect with him.

We did so, and while he took the work and performed his due diligence, he remained somewhat disengaged throughout the transaction. But we had reconnected, and over time our relationship moved from professional courtesy to personal acceptance and, finally, to genuine friendship. He and his wife eventually started attending a Bible discussion in our home, and it was deeply gratifying to play a part in them coming to know Jesus. There was a sense that our relationship—from when we met, to where we were now—had come to the place it was always meant to be.

To us, that was a snapshot of what moving toward the New Normal was all about. We would never have met this attorney without having had the crash. Although it seemed early on that our relationship was purely professional, in the long run our connection led to his deeper connection to God. We watched this man and his wife grow deeper in their love for each other and deeper in their authentic relationship with Jesus. It was a constant reminder of how God works far outside the parameters we might think apply to any given situation.

A few years ago, I received a phone call from this same friend. It was several years after our time at the church, and many years after our reconnection with him and his wife in our discussion group. I noticed an undercurrent of true joy and peace in his voice, and I commented on it to him.

"Well, John, I'd say you're right," he said. "Even though I was fairly successful, my life was not as fulfilled as it could have been. Coming to know Jesus, and growing in a true relationship with Him, has given my wife and me a deeper and truer perspective on life. We've made a decision to pursue things that really matter, not simply things that only outwardly seem to spell success. In fact, that's why I'm calling. I've just been diagnosed with an inoperable brain tumour, and the doctors tell me I have about eighteen months to get my life right. For me, that means reconnecting with the important people in my life, the people who've had a significant impact on the way my wife and I now do life. It's been wonderful. And I just wanted you and Lorraine to know how grateful we are for the role you've played in our lives… in the journey we've been on."

I'd thought my initial connection with this attorney had been about settling Byron's insurance claim, but God had known the relationship was really about him getting the deeper issues of his life settled. It took a while, but in the end this attorney was able to find peace and joy even in the face of his own impending death. Our friend has passed away, but the joy and gratitude in his voice during our last phone call will be with me the rest of my life. That's what embracing a New Normal is all about.

* * * *

I believe each of us is constantly establishing a New Normal in our lives in many areas, although the process is often so subtle that we're hardly aware of it. Only occasionally is the process fast-tracked or intensified because of a cataclysmic event or crisis like ours. Often the smaller, more everyday events are the catalysts for our need to embrace change. We graduate from high school, and then find work or begin college. We marry, and then build a new life with family, perhaps with children. We work hard, and then retire. Life constantly changes—and sometimes change is triggered by events beyond our control, such as a global recession or environmental disaster.

For the longest time, I was looking forward to the day when everything would be stabilized, when we would know exactly what was happening in the long run with Byron. It was a slow-dawning realization for me that the New Normal was not going to be a fixed event. Different personalities respond to their environments in different ways, of course, but I for one was really looking for a time and place where I could stand securely and know exactly what was what in my world. From our regular conversations and prayer times, I knew John was looking for the same.

For example, when Byron finally came home from the hospital, I thought our time of constant flux was ending. It wasn't. When we packed up and headed west, I hoped our new setting would settle us. It didn't. Yes, everything was new and eventually started to seem normal, but there was certainly no settledness in our lives. Then, when we were invited to join the church team back in our former province, I was sure we'd finally landed in the New Normal, and would be set for life. After all, wasn't this an important goal we'd identified years earlier? But again, we hadn't arrived. Many things were new and different, and we had to readapt to our surroundings. We believed this opportunity was exactly where God was taking us, but it seemed that the New Normal was always somewhere out in the future ahead of us.

We found a new home; that change was dealt with. We adapted the home to accommodate special-needs equipment; that change was dealt with. Brent got settled in a new school; that change was dealt with. John and I settled into our new roles in church leadership; that change was dealt with.

But the changes kept coming. Some were big, some were small, and sometimes there seemed to be long stretches between changes. Nevertheless, eventually the need for another adjustment of some kind would make itself known.

From today's perspective, John and I realize that change has always been a part of our lives, and was part of our lives even prior to the crash. Things felt more stable back then, though, and the changes were far less severe than those that arose when we were dealing with life-threatening injuries and the recovery process involved in dealing with a brain-injured son. But that ever-elusive quest has finally brought us to the place where we realize, clearly, that the New Normal is an interior acceptance on each of our parts of the constant change going on around us.

Recently, I was reading from *The Message*, a translation of the Bible I've come to enjoy. I turned toward the back of the book to Thessalonians and read, *"This is why we've thrown ourselves into this venture so totally. We're banking on the living God"* (1 Timothy 4:10).

In short, that's how we live our lives; we move forward relying on God to get us through! For us, the first day of the rest of our lives started the moment we regained consciousness after the crash. At that point, all we could hold onto was Jesus. We knew our old normal had come to an abrupt end, and we were committed to making it to the New Normal, whatever that was for us and our family. By banking on the living God, we knew we could make it through to the other side.

At first, we thought the New Normal was going to be a destination, a place where we'd arrive at one day, a place from which we could start walking forward on solid footing again. But we've come to realize that it's is not a destination, or even a return to where we left off. It is rather a set of constants within an ever-shifting environment—a framework of unchanging principles within a world where nothing is static.

The 9/11 attacks, the growing number of cataclysmic environmental disasters in recent years, the global economic collapse in the fall of 2008… increasingly, we live in a world where nothing remains solid and change is inevitable. That's the New Normal—understanding that everything is changing, and being able to accept that change quickly while moving toward a new reality that we do not yet see.

My security and stability, I've come to realize, simply cannot be placed on any foundation other than God. He is unchanging in a world where everything changes. I can't find security in my husband's strength, because he can be taken from me in an instant—and almost was. I can't find stability in our businesses, because they can fail anytime—and almost did. God is the only constant upon which we can stand for security and stability during incessant change.

The New Normal has nothing to do with stability at all; rather it's about embracing change. Now that we've understood that concept, we see it in application all around us. People who are able to let go of false security and grasp the idea that everything is always going to change are the ones who find strength and the ability to continue growing in a world where everything is new and different all the time.

We've always enjoyed social connections with people. After the crash, though, we were no longer the first ones invited to a party. Our social lives changed significantly. We had a lot to deal with in caring for Byron, so any outing was a major event. People unaccustomed to Byron's interaction with the world were often uncomfortable, not knowing how best to respond to him.

Even though our social calendar was far less full than it had been, we were often called when someone had questions at a heart level. Those deeper conversations filled our often-depleted emotional tanks. We continued to meet with friends one-on-one to hear their stories and encourage them.

The encouragement went both ways; these relationships became a real gift of life to both John and me.

* * * *

Lorraine and I had now become established in our specific leadership roles, and therefore found ourselves fully engaged in church life. Since it was my role as executive pastor to implement board decisions, I was part of the team responsible for soliciting help in moving the church beyond its present static growth. That was our introduction to Dr. Carl George—author, speaker, and also Executive Director of the Charles E. Fuller Institute (CEFI) of Church Growth and Evangelism based in Pasadena, California. Carl and I spent a great deal of time together and developed a strong friendship.

This was a defining time in our ministry journey; we knew God had led us there, but we were pretty sure God was leading us onward, once again—would that leading take us away from the Greater Dream we believed God had placed in us? Knowing, finally, that our New Normal was not a destination, we committed ourselves afresh to the next part of our journey with Him. We accepted that reality, and we tendered our resignations—at the height of our growing effectiveness at the church.

Brent was leaving home that year, and we felt a move would have minimal impact on his life. Byron's health was very important to us, and the cold was definitely taking its toll on him. At the same time, we felt we'd set a precedent years earlier when we chose to bring him home despite the best arguments of experts and others. To us it was already settled in our hearts that what was best for Byron would be of paramount importance to us. We knew that God would continue to show Himself faithful.

Fresh territory beckoned; so did my curiosity. It was the weekend of our staff farewell dinner that Dr. Carl George invited Lorraine and me to meet with him.

Given our history with Carl, Lorraine and I were excited about the meeting.

Carl dispensed with small talk and moved right into his agenda for the evening.

"When I heard you were leaving the church," Carl began, "and knowing God has used both of you in this setting, I wondered if He might be preparing you for something new. We've been tossing around the idea of expansion into Canada, and it seems to me like the two of you could do well in this new endeavour."

Were we ready to take on a new challenge? Was this what we'd been groomed for these last few years? Our excitement grew as we continued the conversation.

"Well, Carl, we are definitely at a place of transition," I told him. "We've had the sense that God was up to something, so we'd be more than interested to speak further with you."

With that, our lives started changing once again. We moved back to the Okanagan Valley and launched a Canadian version of Carl's CEFI ministry. We said yes to him, because we really believed it was part of God's Greater Dream for us. We had difficulty seeing how we were equipped for this new role or how it would unfold, but we moved forward trusting that God and Carl could see the future better than we could! It took a lot of courage and hard work, and a lot of faith, but starting with an office in our home we launched The Leadership Centre, a Canadian presence for the Charles E. Fuller Institute of Church Growth and Evangelism.

The best part for Lorraine and me was the mentoring we received from Carl himself. In ways that reminded us of our time with Terry Winter, Carl poured himself into us, spending time with us in person and on the phone.

He wanted to make sure we were equipped for the challenge, helping us understand and absorb the very DNA and culture of the ministry. In ways that went significantly beyond what was required, this nationally respected leader valued and encouraged us. The importance we place on mentoring to this day was substantially shaped by the mentorship we received from Carl as we worked to grow the organization.

And grow it did. After disconnecting from the American parent group, The Leadership Centre became a standalone entity under Carl's continued supervision. Eventually we amalgamated with the Canadian arm of Bill Hybel's Willow Creek Association, and changed the organization's name to The Leadership Centre Willow Creek Canada.

Once again, we'd found that following God's lead and remaining true to the values that had become central to our lives filled our unwritten tomorrows with more living of the Greater Dream than we would ever have imagined possible! We'd known we wanted to invest our lives into others, and now, through The Leadership Centre Willow Creek Canada, we were pouring into the lives of leaders in churches large and small all across our nation. It was a privilege we never took for granted.

Again we found that our life story provoked quick trust in people we worked with—and trust is a powerful commodity when leadership growth and mentoring is on the table. Person after person began to encourage us to write a book using our story to clarify the values we had learned. And so, that process began to unfold.

*   *   *   *

Our son Brent knew what it was like to have the comfort of normal taken from him at such a young age. While our crash affected him physically for a short time, the longer-term impacts were at a much deeper level. His reality changed drastically from one of normalcy to one none of us could understand.

Brent remembers almost nothing about that era of his life. His natural coping mechanisms sealed off the emotional impact of those months and years so that he could continue to function.

Years later, Brent married a ministry associate, and together they shared a life within local church ministry.

Yet, the broken support systems he had built his life around could not withstand the ordinary pressures that come with a growing family and ministry demands. When the pressure reached its zenith, Brent was ready to reach back, face his present reality of a crumbling marriage, and repair the broken systems, giving strength where it was most needed. His internal and external responses to situations he faced as a grown-up, seemingly unconnected to anything he'd lived through as a child, were actually being fuelled by his unresolved abandonment issues.

Through a focused time apart from everyday life and a deep and real encounter with Jesus—in which he began the process of identifying and dealing with these hurts—Brent found profound and meaningful healing. He identified and dealt with his chronic emotional pain, and continues to this day the process of walking a journey toward wholeness.

Byron was about to experience his greatest post-crash change yet.

As life would have it, even as we write this story, we're still dealing with constant change in Byron's care. We made choices based on medical advice and what was available to us at the time. We reached what seemed to be a plateau for a number of years. Recently, though, Byron has become increasingly less mobile, and our interactions with medical professionals have once again increased.

Around this time, a family friend asked us about some of the care choices we'd made.

"There are other choices available," she said, and then told her personal family story. When I heard her story, even after all these years, I could see we still had unexplored ground to cover with Byron.

"After the crash we pursued every avenue of therapy open to us," I told this friend. "Byron has continually been in speech therapy, in physiotherapy, in therapeutic horseback riding, and in any other therapy that seemed as though it might make a difference."

For a span of time, we no longer pursued new avenues; we simply lived in the ways that had become normal for us. But now we were standing face to face with this new crisis, Byron's decreasing mobility, and it looked like once again we'd have to expand what we knew as normal to include other treatments, like the ones our friend described. We looked into these other treatments and, as a result, began going through a fresh season where everything seemed unstable again.

It's been quite unnerving how much this past season has mirrored those early years in rehabilitation. We've been spending a lot more time taking Byron to medical specialists in different cities, watching to see whether or not all the effort will make a difference.

Certain realities have really hit home. While most of our friends were enjoying a restful, relaxing summer, we were taking disconcerting trips down memory lane. The feelings of déjà vu caused us to relive the pain, fear, and uncertainty of our early years after the crash. We spent a lot more time in the ER, and made endless doctor visits and trips to the hospital for medical tests. We actually noticed improvements in Byron's cognitive abilities, or at least in his ability to express his thoughts more clearly.

As we embarked on writing this book, we came to experience more change than we've seen in two decades. It's as though God wanted to remind us of the things we've been through and are now writing about. It seems He is again expanding our life experience, making us better able to walk alongside others dealing with harsh realities. We don't know where this journey is taking us, but I'm reminded that my part is to embrace the change quickly, and to trust God when I cannot see; His part is to keep pointing me in the right direction.

*   *   *   *

Even in our professional lives, our New Normal was never a place to settle down and stay awhile.

Once again we were given an opportunity to live out that reality. As we wrote, we felt God's hand nudge us again. But instead of feeling validated, we felt uneasy. It became clear that we couldn't rest in the security of the familiar, as comfortable as we thought it was. We were writing about the need to embrace change as part the New Normal, about always persevering and pushing on for the Greater Dream, and now we stood face to face with a huge challenge: to step out of our roles at The Leadership Centre Willow Creek Canada and face an unknown future.

To say this turn of events was significant would be an understatement, yet we came to see that any other choice would have kept us from the Greater Dream—that life for which God had prepared us.

Again, normal for us is accepting change. We're giving our hopes, dreams, and ambitions to God, whom we've learned can be fully trusted. No, the future is not clear, but we're excited that God still has unexplored territory for us to walk into.

During our final years with The Leadership Centre Willow Creek Canada, God gradually opened our eyes to a new reality. Conversations with leaders revealed their growing dissatisfaction with the modest change they were seeing in the lives of those under their guidance. Many times, we heard their longing for encounters with Jesus that would transform the lives of those who follow Him.

Up to this point, our focus had been on leadership, on walking with church leaders in their quest for organizational and spiritual growth. Now God was turning our focus inward, yet expanding our reach to include the entire body of Christ. He was up to something new, and strategically placing change in our lives once again.

Our new ministry—called Encounter God—has now moved into the western regions of Canada. Encounter God allows us to invest our unwritten days into those who desire more from their spiritual experience. Time after time, we've come into contact with people from all walks of life who are no longer content to experience spirituality in a shallow, status quo way, in a way apart from the pursuit of knowing Jesus intimately. Brent expressed this well when he recently said, "I grew up in a Christian home, I attended Sunday School, I learned the Bible verses, I attended church throughout my high school years, and I even went to Bible school, but when I turned twenty years of age, I realized Jesus and I were still strangers."

When the desire for more of Jesus takes hold in our lives, we are able to let go, submit everything to Jesus, and encounter Him in a fresh, deep, and life-giving way. In the end, our lives are radically changed.

Eleven months into this new phase, God gave us an encouraging glimpse of the picture He'd seen all along. In response, we planned for our first Encounter God Retreat. It was clear we were not to publicly promote the concept or the event, but rather invite the people God brought our way. In turn, they would form a team to take the movement forward.

The experience was more than we could have imagined. Jesus' love and healing touch dramatically impacted the lives of those who participated. We were reminded of the words in the Bible of prisoners set free, captives released, and broken hearts healed. Life change became the mark of success, and we stood back and watched in awe.

Now we see the future with a little more clarity, yet many questions remain: How will we fund this venture? Will we need to move across the country, or beyond? How will we get the message out? Despite these questions, we've seen and experienced God in a new way. We're excited about the future and content to allow God to lead us along a pathway of fuller trust than we have ever walked previously.

*   *   *   *

John has always been fond of saying, "You only get to do this life once; there are no internships or reruns." And it's true. What we learn in one season of life prepares us for the next. We also know full well that we'll walk with a limp as we move on in our journey, but we will carry on pouring ourselves into this venture of life, counting on the living God. It's the only way to go.

Crazy as it may seem, we're actually still excited to see how the next season will unfold. We know the plans we see emerging will require deep commitment, and we're excited that our son Brent and his wife Sabrina are walking with us in this new venture. We've seen Brent grow to be resilient and increasingly centred in the last years, dealing with what life has thrown at him. We've seen some of that in each other, too. Strangely, we've also learned that it's not our resilience or persistence that keeps us on track, but rather our brokenness and dependence on God.

Musings

CHAPTER 11

PAST REDEEMED

The good things we write into our lives today set up the foundations of our unwritten tomorrows. In the same way, the bad things we—or others—wrote into the script of our lives long ago can continue to impact us today.

That became abundantly clear during a weekend retreat we hosted for mega-church senior pastors and their spouses at a friend's beautiful ocean-front home. The weather had been wonderful. Backlit by the summer sun, the ocean spray looked warm and inviting, which set the stage perfectly for a meaningful and productive getaway.

It was our final morning together, and we'd gathered for our last session of the retreat. I opened with a few thoughts that had struck a deep chord in me when I first heard them earlier in the year from author and speaker Gordon MacDonald: "To live a resilient life, ensure that you keep your past in a current state of repair." It seemed an appropriate message to share with these friends.

I went on to speak of something I'd read about in a Harvard business magazine. In the corporate world, it's common to subject executive candidates to a battery of personality tests to determine their suitability for specific employment. These tests can reveal how things from the past will affect them in the present. Let's say an executive candidate has a "gap" in his relationship with his father because he was never able to please him. Rather than seeing it as a negative issue, some companies actually look for that gap, because it may mean the candidate is a workaholic overachiever—a real asset to the company. Of course, while the corporation may benefit from having driven overachievers on staff, the residual stress and pain in the life of the individual—and in his or her family—can have an extremely negative long-term impact.

I shared insights like this, wanting to illustrate that unresolved hurts and issues from our past can have significant consequences on our present and future. This had been of major consequence in my own life, and I wanted to ensure everyone at the retreat had an opportunity to reflect on that before leaving.

When the retreat ended and each couple packed up and left, Lorraine and I flew directly to another city, where our organization was to host a leadership conference. There was much to do as we arrived at the conference site, so we dove into the work at hand.

The following day, just as I was about to meet the keynote speaker at the airport, my cell phone rang. It was a pastor friend of mine, one of the retreat guests from the weekend before.

"John, I know you're in town, and I must see you!" His tone was urgent. I explained that my time was pretty much spoken for, and that I needed to focus on the conference. His response was blunt. "I must see you tomorrow—this is critical."

Knowing he understood the work involved in hosting a major event, I realized his need was real. I rearranged meetings and committed to seeing him over dinner.

When I arrived at the restaurant, my friend was already seated and waiting. The minute I sat down he began to weep, revealing incredible anguish. A bit at a loss as to what was happening, I quickly moved to his side of the booth and put my arm around him until his sobbing subsided.

I said the first words that came to mind. "Talk to me! What's going down?"

It was abundantly clear that my friend was dealing with a great weight of sorrow. With much effort, he started talking about the retreat we had enjoyed together the previous weekend.

"Your closing words in that last session have been haunting me," he said. "I wanted to speak up at the time, to say my past is definitely not in a current state of repair, but I could not put into words the horror of my life. I wanted desperately to speak up, to admit and face the dark places in my life, but I didn't know who I could trust." He hesitated. "As a pastor, my life simply does not measure up to my words."

My friend spilled the story of what had been going on. He'd arrived home from the retreat to a phone call from the chairman of his church's board, who reported that a woman had accused him of having an ongoing sexual relationship with her. Although the affair was now over, the woman was overwhelmed with guilt. She wanted to pursue wholeness and healing, part of which involved bringing the truth to light.

My pastor friend admitted the validity of the story, and with great pain told me that his eleven-year, highly effective career in this particular church was swiftly unravelling. He understood why, and accepted responsibility for his actions.

We talked and prayed together, and he acknowledged that as close as we'd been as friends, he still hadn't felt safe enough or desperate enough to talk with me about his situation until the house of cards started to collapse all around him.

Since our restaurant conversation, the unwritten story through which my friend is now walking has played out in divorce, with all the pain that brings. Needless to say, his position as founding pastor of a highly-respected church plant is now history. It's hard to explain the blanket of bewilderment and disillusionment that has been thrown over the people once shaped by this man's spiritual leadership.

As I sat with my friend in the restaurant that day, he unfolded a bit of his formative story with me. He'd grown up in an abusive home, fathered by a man who had little value for him. His mother eventually left her husband and immigrated with her son to Canada. As a teenager wrestling with the impact of abuse and a broken home, he found himself on the streets of Montreal immersed in the drug and alcohol culture. One night, after a few years in the inner city with no real direction or purpose to his life, he took a drug overdose that should have ended what he considered to be his meaningless existence.

When he awoke and found himself still alive, my friend set out to continue wandering the streets with no particular destination in mind. There was music rolling faintly down one city corridor; feeling strangely drawn toward it, he set off down the street in search of the music's source. It turned out to be coming from a church.

Quietly and unobtrusively he slipped in, taking a seat in the very last row of seats. Compared with the turmoil in his soul, the atmosphere in the church was peaceful and steady. He allowed himself to relax into whatever was going on. As the service continued, he started hearing truth he'd never encountered before—truth that resonated deep within his broken soul. He found himself drawn to the warmth of love and acceptance. At seventeen years of age, he was introduced to the person of Jesus Christ for the first time, and made a commitment to follow Him.

Combined with his natural gifts and abilities, my friend's newfound decision, coupled with his desire to "give back," set him on the fast track to a life of leadership and ministry. He soon married, pursued relevant schooling, and marked out a path of service and dedication. At that point, his story was a real page-turner.

The more we talked in that restaurant, though, the more I realized that what he'd said in his opening statement was chillingly accurate: his past definitely was not in a current state of repair. Although seemingly committed to God from his teen years onward, his residual childhood pain and addictive behaviour patterns, as shown by the extramarital affair, were a current reality. He'd never received the help he needed to work through the issues that kept him from living in wholeness and fullness.

As unfortunate as it may seem, this is merely one story among many. Highly gifted leaders with great potential suddenly leave their posts or spiral out of control into immoral or destructive trajectories when their past shows up with a vengeance to take them out. Lorraine and I have come to believe it's not *if* your past will suddenly reappear and knock you off the rails, it's *when*—unless there's been an intentional pursuit of healing and wholeness.

This message, more than anything, is what compels us to speak up and do what we do. If we have spent years living with unresolved past issues, the subplots those issues have written into our lives will eventually show up. They will either limit our effectiveness or drag us through their horrific consequences unless we walk through the process of intentionally rewriting the negative impact those issues have had on us.

Nothing will derail us from the pursuit of our Greater Dream faster or more powerfully than unresolved issues from the past. We believe strongly that the key ingredient in working through these dream-wreckers and life-killers is an encounter with the living God, who alone has the power to take us through genuine healing. Inviting Jesus into those deep places, and hearing His words of love and affirmation, enables us to overwrite the negative past with His message of truth.

It's not always a sudden cataclysmic event that knocks us off-track. For many of us, it's a slow burn. John Ortberg refers to it as a "shadow mission" that controls our lives. We each have a Greater Dream we are built to pursue, a passion and focus in life which ideally can impact others and make a difference for the greater good. It is what we would call one's "life mission." When we have inner drives which are off-kilter, because of hurts and unresolved past issues, our life mission—our Greater Dream—can become subtly hijacked by this shadow mission. Our daily energy and activities, and even long-term pursuits, can become more about satisfying this shadow mission than about living out the Greater Dream. The unwritten portion of our lives, the untapped future with its potentially endless possibilities and op-portunities, becomes restricted and shaped by the shadow-mission writing we are doing each day.

My feelings of lack when I compared myself to my gifted older sisters shaped me early on to be driven and competitive. Left unresolved, that per-ceived gap blossomed into a shadow mission that drove my personal and professional decisions for years. I delighted in proving that I could do what people said could not be done. I relished any chance to prove I could make a difference.

While I accomplished a great deal, to a great extent my journey was more about pursuing the shadow mission of demonstrating my worthiness than it was about living the Greater Dream. "Proving myself" meant being seen as "having what it takes," whatever that meant. In contrast, pursuing the true Greater Dream, for me, is about making a difference in the lives of others—for their sake, and for the sake of their own Greater Dream.

Had I not allowed God to step in and do His work of healing, I would have been on a life trajectory which could eventually have seen me spiral out of God's purpose for my life. The crash would probably have resulted in a complete crisis of faith, because my ability to accomplish anything was obliterated during those long months of rehabilitation. The crash didn't build character in me so much as reveal the work I'd allowed God to accomplish in me up until then.

I said I'd allowed God to step in and do His work, but in reality I was strong-willed, set in my ways, and determined to prove myself until I had been challenged often enough—by scenarios such as my interaction with Chuck Colson's director—to let God accomplish what He wanted to accom-plish in me.

A pertinent example from my own life is the difference between when we'd first had the thought of hosting outreach barbecues and when we ac-tually began hosting them. In the initial stages, I worked hard, and pushed even harder, just to get the idea established. I was driven enough to head to Washington to enlist Chuck Colson. In contrast, when we actually began hosting the barbecues later, the idea almost drifted into place of its own accord. The people in our discussion group worked as a team to own the concept and deliver the product. Even the selection of the first guest speaker, Terry Winter, was clear because he'd become the catalyst for the group.

Same goal. Different approaches. Had the barbecue project proceeded by my efforts alone, it would have come to a crashing halt after our accident. I wouldn't have been there to push it through. As it was, though, the barbeques continued because they were part of the Greater Dream for each of us in our discussion group; it was not just my agenda. Everyone valued the difference it made in people's lives, and together they committed to keeping the dream alive.

To me, that example shows clearly the contrast between leadership and accomplishment built on drivenness—which would have been evidence of my own unresolved past issues—and leadership built on the healthy foundation of a life of wholeness. The level of activity might be the same, but the motivations, foundations, and ways in which the activity is carried out are vastly different. The barbecues were fruit grown from a tree planted in healthy soil—longer lasting and more nutritious than fruit from a tree growing in unhealthy soil. Unresolved issues make for very unhealthy soil. We are held captive by our past issues. Unless we work through them, we continue to write them, albeit unknowingly, into the foundation of our unwritten tomorrows.

Our ability to live out the Greater Dream we are built for is diminished and even potentially sabotaged by these shadow missions. My pastor friend had made a genuine and truly life-changing commitment to God, but even so, his past issues reared up and bit him when the pressures of leadership and acclaim started to build. When the stress intensified, everything he had built crumbled like a house built on a foundation of sand.

I've seen the impact of this on others who are close to me, although all our stories and issues are unique. Parts of my life that need the powerful touch of Almighty God may not even show up on the radar for others. In the same way, issues others find crippling may not even register with me. The important thing is that we each look at our own lives, our own issues, and take the steps necessary to bring healing and restoration to our souls. Only then can we write the stories of our unwritten tomorrows on clean paper.

Sometimes the issues are extremely subtle in the way they lodge in our spirits. They never make themselves known as specific thought patterns that we can notice and pull out by the roots, but they can still work their influence on our daily decisions and actions.

Lorraine and I see these scenarios play out again and again in the lives of men and women around us, leaders and non-leaders alike. The media often reports stories of sudden, catastrophic meltdowns in the lives of recognized public figures whose indiscretions have destroyed their families and professional lives. Many times, the tragedy is less dramatic, although just as impacting. Real men and women who could be living the Greater Dream have settled for less, held captive by issues from their past—consciously or unconsciously—which hobble them and keep them tethered far below the potential they were designed to explore.

Again, I am reminded of the words spoken by Gordon MacDonald: "If you want to live a resilient life, keep your past in a current state of repair." Lorraine and I would tweak that to say, "If you want to live your Greater Dream, let Jesus step into your past and heal the pain and unresolved issues hidden there."

Only then can you move forward to a place of real hope.

Musings

CHAPTER 12

PEOPLE MATTER

Attending the funeral of someone like my dad—who'd lived a long, full, and meaningful life—can be looked at as a celebration of sorts. The event was not filled with gaiety and laughter, of course, but there was honour and recognition for a job well done, plus countless memories from family and others who'd been privileged to know him.

The bumper sticker that says "He who dies with the most toys, wins!" is so obviously ignorant it's laughable. We all know that the number of possessions one has does not constitute success or failure in life, yet sometimes even the best among us live as though what we own or what we accomplish is the marker of whether or not we've made it. The end of one's life, though, has a way of refocusing us on the truth, that it is highly relationships and human connections which matter most. Every individual who enters our life matters.

One thing we gradually realized after the accident was our need for others. John had always been a go-getter who made things happen, and I, too, had been very self-sufficient, wanting to pull my own weight and carry my own load. Our immediate tendency post-crash was to let the doors close behind us and to remain safe in the confines of our home, to fall back on our own strengths and rebuild by ourselves. The shift we faced was subtle, yet enormous: to simply survive as people, and then as a family, we had to become willing to depend on the help of others.

Over the months, as we reframed our experience and cracked open the door to a future we could not comprehend, our need for people grew. Our inability to move forward without the kind and gracious help of others confirmed in us this need to live and move in community rather than in isolation. We simply could not move forward in our own strength—we needed others.

In contrast to the well-wishers who actually provided us with non-support through unsolicited advice and opinions, there were people who gave so much and encouraged us so often that they truly made a lasting impact. Without the medical personnel, we literally would not have survived. And without the help given so willingly by family and friends, we would probably not have survived as a family, and would almost certainly not have been able to get back on the journey of living out our Greater Dream.

Some people come into our lives for a while, and others for a lifetime, yet they all have an impact. Although it took time, John and I have come to believe that God has given us relationships to be held as a sacred trust. A wise older man once told us, "Never burn a relational bridge; over time, most relationships will come full circle." When you live long enough, you see that played out time and again.

This was not an insight that came easily. In moments of reflection, I've noted the many times we've allowed the people God brought us to simply drift away again, much like holding sand in your hand and feeling the grains sift through your fingers. It's a lifelong challenge, it seems, to learn how to hold relationships firmly yet tenderly. They can be so fragile.

I'd always assumed, for example, that family connection and mutual support was normal. But when crisis hit and life came apart at the seams, I was shown clearly that family and friends are gifts to be treasured. For a long time, we couldn't give back in the normal give-and-take way, and yet those around us kept giving, not expecting anything in return. At times we felt overwhelmed with guilt that we could not give back as we felt we should.

Apart from my sister Carol, who delayed her plans to move to Austria so she could be by my side, other family members jumped into action in the same way, one by one stopping by the small town where I was in hospital, and then travelling on to the city to be with John and the boys. My brother and John's sister were among the first to arrive, along with another sister of John's and her husband, who lived nearby. My four younger sisters, who lived in the same province, soon arrived to help, as did John's sisters, one from the Vancouver area, and the other from Washington, D.C. Full of energy, they were eager to help in any practical way they could.

John's mom was less mobile than our siblings, and seemed to turn grey overnight in response to the shock of what had happened, but she quickly committed to fighting for us in prayer every day. Each week she called, pen and paper ready, to ask how she could best pray for us that week.

I sometimes wonder whether, if left to ourselves, the majority of us would choose to live in our own little worlds. Some of us are truly social people; online networks like Facebook and places like Starbucks testify to the human desire for interaction. Yet that connection occurs more often in computer and commercial venues than it does in living rooms and kitchens and front porches, like it used to.

Deep need has a way of opening us up to community. We are pulled, sometimes kicking and screaming, from self-sufficiency to insufficiency— from being complete on our own to needing what others can bring to us or do for us.

Each day of our lives we're living out the consequences of choices we've made previously, just like we're writing the foundation today of what will form our unwritten tomorrow. For the Baergen family, once we lost our ability to function as an independent unit, our extreme need caused us to consciously write in those connections with other people.

I remember one time when John and both boys were still in the hospital and I was in my little apartment nearby. I was overwhelmed by my sense of aloneness, of being left to face the big, unknown world all by myself. It was terrifying. I called my sister Verda, who lived about three hours away, and asked if she'd come spend the weekend with me. I didn't need to persuade her; she jumped on the bus and was with me later that same evening.

When it came time for Brent to leave the hospital, we had no way of providing what he needed—but extended family members were able to provide that important place of connection, safety, and fun. When Byron came home from the hospital, one brother-in-law built a ramp that enabled us to wheel his chair into the house. Another brother-in-law built an ingenious contraption that helped Byron stand safely for longer periods. It sported a desktop out front on which he could write and draw and hold books; it latched behind him so that he was held up safely. We will never forget how these people stepped up to our empty plates and nourished us during these difficult times.

As the months passed, we began to think beyond the parameters of crash and injuries and focused on the reality of making a living. I knew I needed to accompany John on occasion to out-of-town meetings, yet this meant having someone to care for Byron. My youngest sister, Terri, made a critical choice to move beyond her own interests and desires and stand in the gap for us many times. Her commitment to Byron has stood the test of time; to this day, there is a special bond between the two of them.

We had no way of knowing before the crash how desperately we'd need these people's love and support. The relationships we had with them, family and friends alike, had been cultivated over years, and when our need arose they stepped forward boldly. I can see very clearly now that the choices we made in writing strong relationships with family and friends in the earlier chapters of our lives came back to us in the form of needed support in these uncharted and unwritten post-crash chapters.

This gift, the people in our lives, is one of the strong values that keeps us on track for living out the greater purpose for which we were created. It's no longer about being the one-person superhero; we were meant to live in community, where encouragement and support are part of the daily equation. There were times when the depth of pain was so great that it made us virtually catatonic, unable to respond to what was required of us. It was then that our need for the community of people around us became so strong that it drew us out, forcing us to think and move beyond ourselves. Only when we embrace the strengths of others to cover our own areas of weakness, and in turn allow our strengths to cover their weaknesses, can we fully engage in life and live out that greater purpose for which we were built.

We learned that truth through many people: the Klemkes, who invited me to live with them during the critical days after the crash, and who remain friends to this day; my mother, who said early on that she'd be there for Byron as long as God kept her healthy (and who's been faithful to her word); Dr. Mabbot, who stood by, day after day, to keep us informed about all that was happening; Del and Jane McKenzie, whose quiet presence and refusal to give advice was such a strong support; Bill and Karen, our farm manager and his wife, who cared so deeply and always stepped in; and our friends from the home group—John and Judy, Gerald and Kathy—who would arrive at our house before church to stay with Byron while we attempted to bring some normalcy to Brent's life. All these people, and others, were a strong backbone for us when we could not stand on our own. We will be eternally grateful to God for His gift of people.

Need has a way of opening us up to community. Whatever personal reticence we might have had toward being a burden on others was obliterated by the extremity of our need. At a time in our lives when it was literally impossible for us to give anything back, we were forced to learn how to receive from others. It changed our world, and a deep and lasting value formed in us to live out the rest of our lives the same way—embracing community, and being lovers of others in practical and heartfelt ways.

After a certain point of recovery, Byron's needs seemed to plateau—unlike the rest of us, whose dependency on others diminished as our physical improvement grew. We then shifted some of the responsibilities for Byron's care onto others who could help in ways we couldn't. We hired a job coach, whose role it was to enhance the quality of Byron's life physically, emotionally, socially, and spiritually. By this time in his progress, Byron was able to communicate, and it was very clear to all around him that Byron's faith was the foundation for any hope in his future.

Over the years, Byron has had many coaches. One who really stood out was a young man named Denny, who'd responded to an ad we placed in the local newspaper. Denny arrived for his first interview in a flashy, high-end Ford half-ton truck. He'd been a pro football player, starting with the Montreal Alouettes and then playing with the Calgary Stampeders and the B.C. Lions. But Denny's time with the Lions was cut short by a career-ending injury. He responded to our ad right when he was freshly dealing with the death of his football dream. Perhaps that's what endeared us to each other so quickly—we each knew what it was like to have hopes and dreams for the future lie broken on the sidelines.

Denny coached Byron for about eight months, and their relationship grew into a deep friendship. When it came time for Denny to head back to Montreal, Byron felt a huge loss. Occasionally, business would take us out east, so when we had opportunity to visit Montreal we'd stop in to visit Denny. Those times were real highlights for Byron whenever he was with us.

On one such occasion, we called ahead to see if Denny could visit with us. Strangely, his phone was disconnected, so we called his mother to get a new phone number. To our utter shock, she told us that Denny had died suddenly of a heart attack.

Needless to say, John and I were extremely saddened by the news, but Byron was devastated. He lay on his bed for the rest of the day just listening to music. It was clearly an incredible blow to him to lose his friend this way. Only when we insisted he come with us to the Saturday night church service did he move off his bed and step out of the despondency that enveloped him.

As we drove home that evening, Byron suddenly broke the silence with words that startled us.

"I'm such a loser," he said, from out of the blue. I swivelled around in my seat and asked him why he would say that. "Because Denny did not know Jesus."

After a silence, during which John and I both swallowed the lumps in our throats, we explained to Byron how none of us could really know whether Denny ended up knowing Jesus or not—in his final breaths, knowing what was happening, he might have made a decision to turn to Jesus. (Later we learned that Byron had, indeed, talked with Denny regularly about Jesus, and that some of Denny's fellow football players had been engaging him in conversations along those lines as well).

Denny was a true gift to Byron, and to us as well. We believe, and so does Byron, that God placed Denny in our lives for that brief time as a gift of encouragement. But in looking at the bigger picture, we also believe God used Byron to invest into Denny's life at a time when he, too, was facing the death of his dream.

After a while we started to realize that the God-silence we had been experiencing for so long was finally starting to dissipate. As our spiritual paradigm shifted, we began to understand that His love, concern, and thoughts toward us were being expressed through the lives and actions of the loving family and friends who were caring for us so practically and deeply. While it'd been easy for us to know what *wasn't* from Him—when people who didn't understand tried to give us advice—we now realized that we *were* hearing God, and experiencing His touch, through these loved ones. It was a slow dawning realization, but it certainly went deep when we got it, and it provided the forward momentum we needed in our journey toward a New Normal.

Gradually, as recovery shifted to "What's next?", we found the Greater Dream resurfacing in our hearts and minds—that desire to give back where we had received so much. Making a difference in the lives of others became paramount in our thoughts. It was like our reserve tanks were being filled again, and those foundational thoughts we'd written into the story of our lives before the crash were once more showing up in our hearts and lives. The kindness, love, and generosity of those who'd walked alongside us had continually rubbed off on us, and it had left a mark.

Slowly but surely, our focus was shifting from ourselves and our recovery to the lives of others who could use a word of encouragement or a touch of love. Through our pain-filled experiences, we developed a new sense of compassion and value for the people God placed in our lives. We began to see that the gift of love and care we extended to them would be wrapped in memories of when we'd been in that place and someone had modelled that care for us.

The work of mentors in our lives started showing its fruit again. Before the car wreck, Dr. Terry Winter had believed in us and mentored us, coaching us through experiences that shaped us for a life of greater investment in people. Once we saw the positive impact the barbecues had been having, we knew we had to continue building into others. Terry would drop us into additional situations, too, where we had to move beyond our comfort zones. He empowered us to think bigger, reach farther, and dig deeper into our faith. Everything he'd written into our lives was resurfacing as we walked through these unwritten days.

The impact of our pastor Del McKenzie continued to see fruit in our lives, too. We'd known his deep, quiet support right from those early hospital days—putting meat on the bones of things we'd heard him teach on Sunday mornings. He, too, was a mentor who made a difference in how we stand, even now, with those whose experience includes pain.

John likes to say, "People are a gift from God; handle with care." We learned that no matter how incongruous or insignificant a connection may seem at the time, we should never underestimate the power and importance of friendships or relationships. The gift of people has a way of going on and on.

The silence was lifting, and it was the people God had brought into our lives who helped lift it. Had we let those relationships fall through our fingers, we might never have known the breakthrough we longed for. But as we embraced the people God brought to us, the clouds began to show cracks of blue around the edges. We knew the winds were changing.

We grew stronger emotionally and spiritually. We continued writing new lessons into the book of our lives during those dismal days, and those life lessons gave us a fresher and deeper perspective on how we could again focus on the Greater Dream for which we were built.

But even the Greater Dream can be sidelined.

Musings

CHAPTER 13

BENT OR BROKEN

Resilience. Strength. Those are good things, right? Don't we all want to get to the place where the storms of life no longer bring us to the brink of collapse, where we can stand strong and live to fight another day?

I could paint other word pictures, but I think my point is clear. Our current culture teaches us that being strong and self-sufficient is a primary state of being that we should aspire to. Yet there are ways and means by which we strengthen ourselves, or believe we are strengthening ourselves, that can actually prevent us from functioning at our best and living out our Greater Dream. In our quest to become strong, we miss out on the opportunity for God's strength to work in and through us.

I can remember clearly as a young boy running around outdoors, exploring the area behind our family house. Way out back was a grove of cottonwood trees; in the springtime when the leaves were out, the whole grove was a fantastic playground, with pathways and routes winding between the trees.

As the only boy, and the youngest in the family, it was sometimes hard for me to hold my own. The cottonwood grove was a great equalizer, though, and I took advantage of it whenever I could. Sometimes I'd be running with my sisters, but more often than not I'd be running *away* from them, because of some new means by which I'd learned to annoy them. In either case, it didn't take me long to learn that if I grabbed a supple branch on my way past one of the trees, and held onto it until it was bent tight, I could let go at just the right moment and it would snap back and inflict serious pain on whoever was chasing me. That quickly evened out the playing field.

I also learned that if I held onto the branch too long, or pulled it too hard, it would simply snap and break, making the branch useless as a tool for inflicting pain.

With negative circumstances pulling on us, and unresolved issues from the past adding to our stress levels, we can let ourselves become bent—pulled down more tightly inside than a branch in the hands of a ten-year-old boy. We've likely all been there, and we've probably all dealt with others in whom the "bentness" has become dangerous—where their pain causes them to snap back unexpectedly and viciously, causing deeper pain to themselves and others than a cottonwood branch ever could.

I had breakfast with a friend the other day. Lorraine and I have often had wonderfully deep spiritual conversations with this man and his wife—but this day things were different. He had owned multiple revenue properties, lived in multimillion dollar homes, ridden the wave of the boom... but now things had changed. Demand for his business had been in steep decline for months, and he was feeling the squeeze.

There had always been such generosity in his life. He'd given large cheques to his favourite charities, dropped tens of thousands of dollars into the offering plate, and taken teams of people to other countries to expand their awareness of world missions.

Financial freeze on its own isn't enough to cause bentness, but the financial freeze seemed to have convinced my friend that God was really letting him down. I have to admit, I was surprised when this once gregarious man spoke with anger and resentment at our breakfast meeting, freely expressing that God owed him and wasn't holding up His end of the deal. I saw seeds of bitterness taking root.

More than anything, it seemed to be a sense of entitlement that was bending my friend down. He seemed to be saying that his performance and generosity had entitled him to certain levels of favour from God, and the failure of God to keep on delivering the appropriate level of favour was tantamount to betrayal. He was bent! I distinctly got the feeling that soon, when it was unleashed, someone was going to feel the sting of it.

In contrast, people who have lived through pain or tragedy and have allowed themselves to be broken and vulnerable—letting the strength of God be their source of life—are often ones who exude safety and peace. They draw others to themselves without even trying, because those who come in contact with them see the essence of God shining through the broken places; there's an attractiveness in the vulnerability.

A few days before that meal with my friend, Lorraine and I spent the weekend with a group of leaders. We'd drawn away from our normal lives for a few days to get quiet and connect with one another. During that time away, we witnessed one of the most genuine examples of true humility and brokenness I've ever seen. One of the leaders opened up about some deep resentment he'd cultivated years before, and shared how Jesus had walked alongside him in the process of shedding that resentment through an experience of genuine brokenness.

A new pastor had come to the church where this man led on a worship team. One thing led to another, and he was gradually excluded from the passion of his life—leading in worship and music. He was so offended that he left the church, drawing into himself and stewing on his own for a long time. Eventually, though, he caught a glimpse of how bitter he'd become. He realized his unforgiveness was leading him down a path that, if lived out, would take him where he knew he did not want to go.

Through a series of events, this man found himself seated in the same church he'd left. In response to the strong prompting of Jesus, he quietly, but with great emotion and determination, released the pain and disappointment he'd held onto for so long. His encounter with Jesus that day was so profound that he made a defining decision: even if he never again lived out his passion of leading worship, it was worth it to give up his "right" to be bitter and angry and walk into freedom.

It took courage for this leader to be vulnerable, but the warmth and acceptance he experienced from the other leaders in the room exemplified how brokenness invites others into a deeper level of authenticity. We felt humbled by our friend's trust and vulnerability, and each of us was inspired to look inward and evaluate our own lives.

The stark contrast between this man's state of being and my business friend's state of being could not have been more dramatic. Within a few days of one another, I had seen two men clearly illustrate the chasm that exists between walking bent and living broken.

Being bent is not completely unfamiliar territory to most of us. Something will go wrong with our day—a minor irritation or an unexpected change in plans—and we start to grumble, either to ourselves or to others. A little later, another irritation or disappointment might present itself, and rather than processing it and moving on, we add it to the first.

At that point, our internal antennae can actually become attuned to "bad stuff," making us more receptive to perceived insults or to the universe "conspiring against us." Without realizing it, we make agreements with the enemy (or the diabolical, as some might say), and an emotional and spiritual downward spiral begins. This agreement continues to shape our thinking as we move forward. We can eventually begin to mistrust people, expect bad things to happen, and if the process goes all the way we might even give up on God and question the very values that form the foundation of our belief system and our lives.

That's different from the broken branch that has lost all its pain-causing power. The broken branch initially suffers the same pulling pressure as the bent branch, but in breaking it releases all the pent-up energy, leaving nothing with which to snap back or strike out at an innocent passerby. Same situation, different result.

Even on a normal day, this getting bent into the wrong shape can happen fairly quickly, and if someone around us happens to walk into our pathway at the wrong time, they end up feeling the sting of our bent branch snapping back. However, if we just as quickly come to a realization of what's going on inside ourselves, we can take away the sting potential before lashing out. But what happens to a life lived with the bentness adding up and never being dealt with?

Perhaps a personal or family tragedy set the process in motion. Maybe there was an insult that lodged deep, or a series of events that led to the death of a dream. Whatever it was that started us down this path, what happens if we allow ourselves to become bent, without ever stopping to understand what's happening inside and allowing the hurts to be healed?

In the weeks following Byron's discharge, the reality of life in our home continually reminded me of the psychologist's comments. All I could see was the bad in everything. I became negative and sullen, and the people around me—Lorraine most of all—received the brunt of my suppressed disappointment and growing bitterness. Even as I continued brooding on the inside, I tried to act normally on the outside, completely unaware of the impact I was having on my family and others.

A person bent in this way will never live out their Greater Dream. They've become stuck to the past, adhered to the person, place, or circumstance that brought the pain. For others, deep-seated regret can become the overriding state of mind, affixed to the memory of how they lived previously or to the situation they feel brought them to that point.

More often than not, when we're bent in this way we cannot see beyond ourselves. We become the centre of our own existence, to put it bluntly. Looking back, I can recognize that my initial focus had been on how this new life situation would impact me and my dreams, not nearly so much on how everything had changed for Lorraine, Brent, or Byron.

None of us are immune to bentness. Life presents us all with enough reasons to warp under the strain. It's our response to those events and situations that determines whether or not we become bent—in other words, what we write into our lives, in those moments, affects how we live beyond them.

The sense of unfairness, of being hard done by, is often what fuels our resilience when we're bent. But that's not the kind of resilience we need; that's the type that feeds upon itself, that gets stronger as it amplifies the perceived wrongdoing. As the feeling of unfairness grows, it's stored as pent-up tension, waiting for the best time to lash out or strike back.

Several years before our accident, when our lives were beginning to blossom and things were coming together for us in good ways, I received a call from one of our church's board members.

"We've received a call from a man who is very angry with you, John," he said. "You've hurt him very deeply, to the point where he says it's ruining his spiritual life." He went on to identify the man and elaborate on his complaints.

I was flabbergasted. I knew who the man was, as we were both in the same church, but had no idea how I'd hurt him or how I could be sabotaging his spiritual life.

"Would you be open to meeting with the board and this gentleman to talk about the situation?" the board member asked me.

"Well, yes, we could meet," I responded, "but I don't know what we'd talk about. I haven't done anything to this man—I don't even know him, beyond a coffee here or there."

"But John, since he feels he's been deeply hurt by you, I'd strongly suggest we meet."

There was a pause while I reflected. "Okay, I accept what you say. I'll be there." I hung up, wondering what this was all about.

That Friday, I came to the church to meet. There were several board members present, our new pastor, and this man. As soon as we got settled, he started to unload. He was the regional sales rep for a home-building company, which meant he was definitely getting beaten up in the marketplace by our company's home-building division. When people compared pricing for a starter home in our target market, we'd usually come in lower than his company. Fair enough; I understood and appreciated his response to being squeezed financially.

But he didn't stop there. For the better part of two hours, he attacked me personally—lambasting me about everything from the type of suit I wore to the kind of cars I drove. And, to top it off, he said I was arrogant.

I was being verbally assaulted, and felt devastated. When would the attack stop?

Finally the board chairman sat forward and brought the diatribe to a close. Looking at the man, he said, "Okay, what do you want John to do about this? What are you asking of him?"

"I want him to apologize for what he's done!"

The chairman turned to me."John, would you apologize to him for what you've done?"

Man alive! He'd assailed me with so many criticisms, how could I pick one to respond to? But I remembered he had called me arrogant, so I figured I could at least respond to that with some measure of integrity. Not surprisingly, I had to dig down really deep, as the words I wanted to use wouldn't have helped the situation!

"I'm so sorry for my demeanour, for what I've done, for the ways in which I've hurt you," I said. "Please forgive me."

The board chairman turned to the man and said, "Will you forgive John?"

The man leaned back in his chair and crossed his arms. "I'll think about it."

For the next thirty minutes, board members redirected the conversation toward the man, challenging him to forgive me and then walk forward into freedom. The meeting finally drew to a close when the man said, "Well, I guess I can do that."

I remember walking out of the meeting wiping tears from my eyes and feeling emotionally spent. I felt so wronged by a man whose jealousy had overwhelmed his thoughts and actions toward my family and me.

The new pastor had followed me out, and he shared his thoughts about what had just happened. "John, I'm so sorry this happened," he said. "It was not something for us to deal with as a board; this was simply a personal vendetta. This should never have happened."

I didn't understand it at the time, but I've come to see I was likely the recipient of the latest snapback from a man whose life was already bent—full of pent-up anger and frustration he hadn't known how to process. Or maybe he just hadn't wanted to. Had he suffered a tragedy in his earlier years? Had he been wronged by someone who dressed like I did? I had no idea what set him on this path, but I sure learned what it's like to be on the receiving end of someone's snapback!

As I've said, bentness shows itself in anger or bitterness, where the snapback is more easily seen and felt in the sting it gives. But bentness can show itself in other ways, too, including serious depression. Lorraine and I have both seen how being bent can wear people down to the point where they're merely surviving, sliding into an existence where they limp from moment to moment. Sometimes even their survival instinct disappears and they give up on life, simply marking time until the curtain comes down.

When bentness manifests in this way, the snapback is often internal, where the one who is bent is the one who suffers the greatest pain. While the people around him may not feel the physical sting of his lashing out, however, they'll still be affected emotionally, relationally, and spiritually. Anyone who has lived alongside someone dealing with depression knows there are many side effects to deal with.

There doesn't seem to be much choice in how it all plays out, does there? Life still happens, tragedy still happens, unfairness or injury or insult or pain still happens; bad things occur in everyone's life at some point or another.

So, is there a choice? Yes. The choice comes right after the pain: are we going to stay bent, or are we going to let go of our rights, accept the reality of where life is taking us, and move forward with freedom and peace? Are we going to hold onto the pain and let the tension of unfairness build up inside and keep all that negative energy building, or are we going to let go of what we thought we deserved and dreamed life would be? It is in that very act of accepting the posture of brokenness where the ability to hurt ourselves and others is dissipated.

On the surface, brokenness might not seem like a very attractive option. When we're bent, close to being broken, it's very hard to see any way out of where we're at. The last thing we want to do is "let go"—if anything, we want to hold on to all we've got with everything we've got!

Isn't brokenness something we're supposed to avoid? If our toaster is broken, that means it doesn't work—it no longer makes toast. If my car is broken, it needs to be fixed. Broken means "not working," right? Or "not together" or "not functioning the way it's supposed to"—that's not something we should *want*, is it?

We're talking about a different form of brokenness. True brokenness is a giving over of the "self-will" portion of our lives. A healthy branch wants to spring back; it's designed to do that. Becoming broken makes the branch unable to exert its will in that way.

A strong stallion can only be ridden when it has been broken. The horse's will is given over to the will of its rider; before that, it's a dangerous animal! Does the horse become any less strong after it has been broken? Not at all— it actually becomes more useful. A broken horse is completely different from a broken toaster.

We believe there's only one true way to be broken, in the healthy sense, and that's to rest all of who we are and what we have—all our dreams and ambitions—on Jesus. It's making a decision to release all our "rights"—all the things we think we're entitled to. At that point, Jesus takes rightful control of our lives.

Untrue brokenness means giving up. "He's a broken man," we'll say, meaning life's pressures were too great and there's nothing left but a shell. In our view, that's like a living branch that's been bent to the point of breaking but hasn't yet snapped. It's still just bowed, not broken, but pretty much bent beyond repair. A branch bent this far will keep growing, but will grow into a new, twisted shape. That's not the brokenness we want.

It's true, of course, that brokenness does not feel like the right way to go, at least not in the beginning. When we talked about this concept to our friend Tim Day, of The Meeting House in Oakville, he said, "When you're broken, you feel like you'll never be used again." And that's absolutely true. Whatever Greater Dream we may have had seems like only a distant memory. Our personal agendas fall by the wayside. We're forced to rely on God to open doors for us, because we cannot even see the doors. All we can see are the walls. And they're closing in.

But strangely, that's when God smiles, because He knows we're giving up on building our own empires. Bent people are frustrated builders; broken people are resting on the strength of the Builder.

When Byron was discharged and I grumbled at the unfairness of life and grieved over the loss of my broken dreams, I was leaning toward being bent for the rest of my life. The crash, however, was not what caused my bentness. Byron's brain injury did not cause it, and neither did the choice we made to bring him home, or the impact that decision had on Lorraine's workload or my business life. None of these things caused my anger, bitterness, and bentness I was stuck in. Each was a reality for me, but the resentment built up in me out of my own choice. Quite simply, the bitterness and anger I felt were my own chosen responses to the realities I was facing.

My dad's twenty-year bout with bitterness was not caused by the financial loss he suffered. It was caused by his own choice to harbour bitterness. "Days turn into weeks, weeks turn into years, and years turn into lifetimes," says pop star Sting in one of his songs. Day after day, Dad chose to write bitterness into the script of his life, and year after unwritten year he reaped what he'd sown.

But somehow during his regular Bible reading that one evening, Dad realized his bitterness would not make things right. Bentness gave way to brokenness as he released his "rights," denounced the unfairness, and then humbled himself enough to apologize and ask for forgiveness. He didn't go seeking justice; he went seeking reconciliation. At that point, Jesus was able to step in and heal the pain he'd held for so many years.

My own freedom came late at night. Lorraine's comment about me losing everything if I wasn't careful cracked through my veneer of self-pity enough for me to see I was helpless to move from where I was without God's help. I had reached the end of myself, and I could either let everything I was so resentful about crush me into permanent bentness, or I could let go of the "rights" I was clinging to. I am grateful beyond description that God gave me the grace to wrestle with Him when I was in that deep abyss of self-pity; His willingness to receive my overwhelming frustration left the door of invitation open to me, and His love drew me back out of my deep self-pity.

In my own strength, I had been fighting back, pushing, snapping out at Lorraine and others as I fought the bending forces converging on me. But when I let go of my own strength—with all my "rights" and painful realities—and simply trusted Jesus again, I snapped like one of those branches back in the cottonwood grove, and my pent-up bitterness, negativity, and self-pity began to fade. To this day, I can still recall the peace and love that washed over me in that moment.

Resilience built with our own strength is debilitating. If it's strong enough, it can foster anger and bitterness under pressure, much like fungus and mould grow in a sealed room as the heat builds. If it's weak, it can lead to a life of weariness, numbness, and depression. Either way, it's built merely on self, and leaves a person incapable of supporting their Greater Dream.

True brokenness, on the other hand, with its complete reliance upon the strength of Jesus, lets the pain of tragedy feed into roots that grow deep. Freedom, joy, and peace replace anger and bitterness, and fresh air blows through the visible cracks.

True brokenness removes the façade. We want others to see us as nice, good, strong, and wise (or strong, wise, good, nice, depending on our personalities). We put up a front when we aren't those things, hoping others can't see through it. Brokenness removes that façade and invites others to see us as we actually are, imperfections and all. That openness and vulnerability can't be sustained with our own strength; it comes only as we allow the strength and love of Jesus to pour into us and shine through our cracks.

I think that's why people seemed to respond so readily to us; they saw the reality of brokenness through our story, and wherever we went it was part of our lives. During our years as part of the church staff, for example, barriers would come down in people we served and we could move into the deeper issues of life.

We've come to understand that, deep down, human beings are all the same. When Lorraine and I stepped out of our comfort zone to accept our positions at the church, we didn't have any energy for building façades. All we could be was our broken selves, and all that sustained us was our dependence on Jesus. When people saw us dealing with life, struggling the same way they did, they felt they could trust us. The responses and deep connections we encountered were from people who were relieved to find us willing to let them in behind the façades.

But what about if we love Jesus? Can people who say their lives belong to Him become bent? If we've experienced true brokenness, can we still become bent again? Does dealing with a challenge always mean we'll become bent?

These are all really good questions. We've wrestled with them as we've explored the concept of being bent or broken. We're not experts, but we have seen things in ourselves and others that provide some insight.

We believe any one of us can be bent. Whether or not we regularly connect with Jesus doesn't seem to matter. Perhaps it *should* make a difference, but I've experienced bentness, and my dad's experience shows that someone who loves God and regularly reads the Bible can still be bent. From what we can see, it always comes down to the question of who is ultimately in charge of our lives at any given moment.

The same holds true for being bent even after we've experienced the surrender of brokenness. We've talked about true brokenness resulting from letting go and allowing God to lead the way forward into an unwritten future. By doing so, the power and sting of the things that bent us are removed. Yet we've both seen people who have truly walked in brokenness suddenly (or gradually) succumb to bentness again. Something caught them off-guard, unconscious agreements with the enemy formed, and before they knew it they became bent.

I believe it has a great deal to do with how we become bent in the first place. The weight of tragedies, difficult challenges, or broken dreams bears down on us, and unless we are vigilant and spiritually aware, self-pity starts to bend us. If we allow that weight to remain, new events, tragedies, or painful situations can simply add to the pile, causing us to become more and more stuck in our bentness.

It's intriguing to realize that we'll remain stuck in our bentness if we simply "add" God to our lives and allow Him to be another piece of the puzzle, as it were, while still holding on to all our pain and questions of "why." If we treat him like a benevolent grandparent who only gives us what we want, or as an insurance policy intended only to protect what we consider important, we actually end up in a posture of bentness, where we can no longer recognize Jesus' voice as He alerts us to follow Him. We can do that even as followers of Jesus, unfortunately, which leaves us open to becoming bent again even after we've been truly walking free.

In brokenness, though, we let go of the pain and baggage which has piled high. In surrendering all our ambitions, hopes, and dreams to Jesus, we allow him to replace the pain with expectancy and security for the future. He then replaces all that dead weight with the freshness brought on by restored hope. The bentness disappears in our brokenness.

In our own lives, and in the lives of those we love, we've seen time and time again that it's only an encounter with the living Jesus that can bring us to that place of surrender. Submitting all of who we are and have to Jesus is a vital part of a true encounter with Him.

But how does genuine brokenness become reality in our lives?

We've seen people experience it in many ways. It can come through God-inspired personal revelation. This is what overtook my father during his regular Bible reading that evening, and prompted him to replace resentment and bitterness with humility and forgiveness. I have no idea how his process unfolded, or how long he'd been pondering things. I'm not even sure what scripture he was reading at the time, but the Holy Spirit was given leeway in my dad's heart that night, and the result was freedom from more than twenty years of bitterness and resentment.

Does a quiet, one-on-one process like that let God's work go deep enough in our hearts to ensure there is lasting change? All I can do is point to the final six years of my dad's life, and the freedom with which he lived the remainder of his unwritten days.

Personal revelation, hearing the voice of Jesus for ourselves, is the point we must ultimately all come to, no matter what first gets our attention. Even God-inspired revelation will have no lasting impact if we don't accept the truth of it and let it settle deeply into our being.

Another means God uses to bring people to an encounter with Himself is through some kind of shock or hard life event. Just as tragedy can set us on the path toward bentness, it can also be the thing that cracks the door open to our need for supernatural intervention. It can be a major event, like an accident or loss, or it can be a minor thing, such as a word someone says or a blurb we hear on the radio. Whatever it is, we're suddenly pausing in our thoughts, giving our head a shake, and thinking through the implications of what just happened.

This is what happened to me. Letting go of my "rights" allowed me to give up on needing to figure everything out for myself, and to move forward in a posture of brokenness.

People also encounter healthy brokenness through help from others. Sometimes we're too stuck in our bentness to be able to come to a place of God-inspired revelation without help. This is one of the many benefits of living in community, of being connected with others on the journey who love us. If we suspect we're walking bent, in any way, we can turn to those we trust and ask them for help. They can help us be honest about things that may be leading us where we don't want to go.

In the end, the brokenness brings one to wholeness. And our lives are radically changed.

*　　*　　*　　*

I don't know why it was this way, but for some reason my Grade Six teacher saw little value in who I was as a young girl, and had no qualms about letting me know—along with implying, in front of the entire class, that I was large for my age. From then on, those thoughts became part of my subconscious identity and left me insecure, believing that everyone around me also saw me as "large."

Only in my adult years, at a weekend retreat, did I become truly aware of that insecurity and the long-term negative impact it had on me—and to see it for what it was. As I identified that these thoughts were actually a lie I had come to believe and accept, I was able to invite Jesus into the whole situation in a fresh way, allowing Him to eliminate the lies and replace them with His truth. For the first time, I was able to understand how God saw me, and on that weekend retreat, so many years after the start of those lies back in Grade Six, I wept deeply as I comprehended Jesus' total and complete acceptance of me... just as I am.

That day, I was given a gift. Through my tears I caught a glimpse of Jesus back in my Grade Six classroom. He walked down the aisle, knelt by my desk, and taking my face in His hands looked into my eyes and said, "I love you just the way you are."

To say the experience revolutionized my life would be to do it an injustice. The past experience, buried in the back of my mind, had shaped my view of how I saw myself and how I thought others perceived me. The issues stemming from my Grade Six year affected my life for years in ways I wasn't even aware of. But Jesus changed all that when I finally understood what was going on and allowed Him to reach in and deal with those issues through His immense love. Now I find myself thinking, had I known the reality of that love back in Grade Six, how differently might I have responded to life?

Brent was, in fact, the first member of our family to connect with Jesus in such a profound way. Before that, he hadn't realized the impact those unresolved abandonment issues were having on his current life. But with the continued help of leaders he met that weekend, he began the journey of severing the ties that bound him—and released the pain, unfairness, and unanswered questions to Jesus.

The results we immediately saw in Brent's life actually became the catalyst for me, as his mother, to encounter Jesus in a similar way. I found tremendous freedom and healing by allowing the more deeply buried issues of my past to be brought to light and be dealt with. Knowing how important that process of revelation and restoration is, I'm now more committed than ever to keeping my past in a current state of repair.

* * * *

Sometimes we need the help of others. Sometimes a sudden event shocks us into a new way of thinking. Other times, God gets our attention through more personal revelation. Whatever the catalyst, our success depends on our willingness to respond.

Peter, one of Jesus' disciples and close friends, encouraged people to rejoice even though they were going through various trials. These trials, Peter said, actually tested the sincerity of their faith, which he said is worth more than gold. The word he chose for "trial" means an experiment designed to prove something, like something a scientist would use to test a theory.

In other words, Peter says our faith is merely a theory until we've walked through the tests that will prove whether or not it's genuine—and this is the same Peter for whom Jesus prayed so that his faith would not fail, right before Peter denied Jesus three times. You'll likely remember that part of the Easter story. Peter could have been bent by his own failure; the text says he went away and cried bitterly. I believe that had he stayed ashamed and bent, his unwritten story would have faded off the pages of history.

However, Peter admitted his failures and trusted Jesus for forgiveness and restoration. Over a breakfast of fish on the beach, Peter later allowed Jesus to bring him to brokenness with three questions. Because of that choice, this same Peter became one of the men who turned the world upside-down with the message of Jesus. Peter knew what it was like to be faced with that choice of bentness or brokenness, and his choice led him to live out the Greater Dream to which he was called.

I'm sure if you asked my sisters about times in the cottonwood grove behind our house, they'd be able to recall what the stinging snap of a cottonwood branch feels like. Like those branches, when we're bent, and choose to remain bent, we have tremendous negative potential to cause pain in our own lives and the lives of others. But an encounter with Jesus can change everything.

The choice of releasing our rights and submitting all we are and ever will be to Jesus is a continual one. Whether we've had major trauma in our lives or are simply dealing with day-to-day irritations, our choice to remain bent or to embrace brokenness is one we write into the story of our lives every day.

The unwritten days we have yet to live will be shaped strongly by those choices.

Musings

CHAPTER 14

FUTURE EMBRACED

When we embarked on the adventure of laying out our life journey in this book, we were settled in most areas of our lives. Byron's health and mobility were comparatively stable, the leadership development group we led was in its seventeenth year, and we were looking forward to continued impact on the local churches in Canada and beyond. Life was good.

Many times over the years we'd been asked to write our story, but the season never seemed right. However, a number of things came together in such a way that encouraged us to believe the time was at hand to see the process through.

What a journey it has been! I don't think either John or I had any idea how painful it would be to walk once more through the details of the crash and our recovery processes. We've relished being reminded of the ways in which God so actively worked in our lives. Re-exploring the life lessons He taught us has brought a new depth to our journey with Jesus. At the same time, thinking so clearly about the deep impact this has all had on Byron, Brent, and others in our lives, has at times brought us face to face with emotions we never thought we'd have to experience again.

Ironically, throughout this time of recollection and reflection, our lives actually seemed to shift back to the post-crash recovery era. After we began the project, Byron was saddled with some major health issues he'd never faced before. Brent, during the same period, experienced a depth of spiritual formation that reshaped his life, restored close family relationships, and even impacted our own spiritual understanding. Both John and I have seen our professional lives radically change from well-established stability to uncertainty yet again.

We sit near the end of our storytelling journey, at least for the territory we've covered in this book. The process has unfolded far differently than we'd originally envisioned, but we're grateful for where Jesus has taken it—even though it's led us down pathways we might not initially have wanted to revisit.

In the foreword of this book, we invited you to journey with us through our story in an attempt to see yours more clearly. We're still on the journey; God continues to deepen our resolve to pursue the Greater Dream. We still want to live our lives focused beyond ourselves, all the while remaining firmly connected to the strength that held John so tightly those many years ago in the hospital.

Where has this journey taken us?

Well, for one thing, the values we've learned—that we've written of in these pages—have been deeply impressed on us through the harshness of our experiences.

We're reminded of the question that was asked of John soon after the car crash: "Do you still believe?" His answer then was, "Yes, quieter but more deeply." Since beginning this journey, a deeper grasp of God's empowering presence has enveloped us. The easily-spoken spiritual comments we might have used earlier in our lives no longer ring entirely true. The depth of our journey has moved us beyond classic Sunday School answers.

We already mentioned my dad's passing. As we stood around his bed—our mom, all of his six children, and two in-laws—we were privileged to witness a transition that will stick with us for life. Dad lived his life as an avid follower of Jesus. His life was marked by a resolve to live his faith despite the challenges before him, and he remained true to that commitment until his final breath.

What we saw in those final moments brought reality to the imagery of climbing the ladder of life. As Dad reached the top of the ladder and peered off into the horizon, he raised his clenched fists and swollen arms, gave a shout, and then breathed his last breath. He saw it! His ladder was firmly in place against the right wall.

We could tell Dad saw what he'd dreamed of seeing—everything he'd committed his life toward. He'd seen that place in his mind's eye over a lifetime, and now he'd arrived. With his faith secure to the end of life here on earth, we saw a profound rest arrive as he stepped across the threshold into eternity.

What a legacy that is as we follow in his footsteps. What a confidence— that the direction toward which we have committed our life will stand the test of time! How could we settle for less than knowing our ladder is up against the right wall, the one Dad directed us to, the one that will hold us strong and take us to that place of eternity with Jesus? How could we settle for less than ensuring that future generations will also be directed to that right wall?

*   *   *   *

At this point in my life, as a father of two and grandfather of three boys, I've been transitioning from leader to the posture of avid learner. In that learning journey, one of my influencers is Brent, who has been teaching and modelling the way along the road for me. His pilgrimage from abandonment toward wholeness has greatly impacted my life. His daily experience in listening to Jesus and seeing the validity of that lived out, has stretched and reshaped my faith. Now it is my grandsons who are giving me the opportunity for a second chance! How amazing it is that God would care about the details of my life to such an extent. The darkness of God's seeming silence those many years ago fades as we experience the joy and expectation of what is yet to come.

Over the past years, I've often been drawn to John 14, where Jesus makes the most astounding statement: *"[You] will do even greater things than these, because I am going to the Father. And I will do whatever you ask in my name…"* (John 14:4, NIV). I have wrestled with these words, and have prayed to understand. I could not see myself doing what Jesus did here on earth, much less greater things. Yet recently, I've sensed that very call on my life: to help men and women, across our country and beyond, leave the captivity of broken pasts and the emptiness of self-absorption and walk into the reality of John 14. What a privilege it is to invite individuals to encounter the living God in their day-to-day lives. Along with that, there's the pure delight of establishing the national expression of the Encounter God ministry in collaboration with our son Brent and his wife Sabrina; I'm amazed and overwhelmingly grateful for that.

But the decision to move in this new direction wasn't an easy one. I'm an entrepreneurial leader, so stepping out of the comfort and acclaim of leading a national ministry—one that we founded—has been more difficult than I ever imagined. It took years to build a solid team, a team that owned the vision with passion and was skilled to fulfill the mission. There was real comfort and security in knowing our team knew how to work together in overcoming any challenges that arose.

The thought of leaving that security to begin again was overwhelming, but God had our attention when stories of leaders who were taken out of the game became personal. We recognized the names and faces of all too many of these gifted and skilled leaders whose inner lives had deteriorated—people living at a level far below their Greater Dream. We could no longer turn a blind eye. God was leading us to a new place of ministry.

With all the uncertainty and discomfort that pursuing a new venture naturally brings, we have become fully immersed in trusting Jesus once again. The stories of life change—of people who'd given up on the Greater Dream, but who now see hope and a new future—give us a glimpse into what Jesus meant in John 14.

We're reminded of our mentor Carl George's words: "Once you have been stretched, you can never go back to your original self." Yes, we are being stretched, and it drives us to trust Jesus more and more. No, we can never go back, nor could we settle for less in our journey with Jesus. We've experienced the reality of God restoring hope when all sense of hope is gone; how could we ever settle for a lesser dream? So, with the words we often say to Byron, we now encourage ourselves: "When you can't see, you have to trust."

*   *   *   *

The summer of this writing could best be described as our summer from hell. Little did we know, as we stepped out of day-to-day leadership at the office, that God would allow a challenge to come our way that would demand our full attention.

Early on that year, Byron fell—his first fall with injury in many years. Within weeks of the first fall, he experienced a second and third fall, all with injury. Trips to the local clinic and then to emergency became normal in those weeks. Then we came face to face with the real crisis: Byron was going blind.

Endless medical consultations and continued trips to emergency could not initially diagnose the problem. Ophthalmologists were already working at capacity, and we couldn't seem to connect with an eye specialist who cared enough to give his time. Then, as only God can arrange, a close friend connected us with a renowned ophthalmologist who agreed to see Byron on two days' notice—and on a Saturday afternoon. The specialist was shocked at the pressure in Byron's eyes, pressure that could blind him irreparably within days. The specialist put Byron on an intense protocol of medication to lower the pressure and, at the same time, scheduled surgery on both eyes for the following day.

Family and friends gathered that evening for prayer. Overnight, the eye pressure dropped to normal levels, and we all hoped God would restore Byron's vision.

Most unsettling, though, was the sense of déjà vu that settled on us. We found ourselves expecting the worst once again. But just as God had placed this ophthalmologist into our lives, he continued to bring people who helped shoulder some of the weight we were carrying.

Byron and I had a recent meeting with a specialist, a neurosurgeon in the town where we live. His office was on the third floor of a building we'd been in before. Normally, that's not an issue; we find the elevator, punch the button, and get out at the right stop. On this visit, though, the elevator was out of commission. John was not with us, so I knew I would have to help Byron up the stairs to the specialist's office. The thought of me supporting Byron up three flights of stairs was overwhelming enough, but at the same time I knew that would be the easy part. I was very glad John would be arriving before we had to go down again.

So we tackled the stairs, Byron and I. He held tightly to the railing and to me. Together we inched our way up the three flights. We finally arrived at the specialist's floor, and made it safely down the hallway to the waiting room.

Once Byron was settled in a chair in the waiting room, I checked in with the receptionist. I explained our predicament and asked if she had any suggestions for our trip back down the stairs. Was there, perhaps, another elevator we could access? Was there any chance the elevator would be fixed before we had to leave?

The young lady's response was curt. She explained the elevator had been broken for a few days, and that, as far as she knew, it wouldn't be fixed until the weekend. No, there was no one she could call, and no, it wasn't really her job to find help for us. Basically, she thought it was my problem, and I would have to deal with it on my own.

Fortunately, John arrived at that point and we settled in to wait for the specialist. The room was full and, as time went by, it seemed the doctor had fallen behind schedule. Even though we were the first appointment that morning, we sat and waited. And waited.

Then John leaned over to me. "Lorraine, I have to go."

I looked at my watch. Sure enough, it was almost time for John's next meeting, which he'd arranged for later in the day so he could be with us for this appointment. We'd spent the whole time in the waiting room without seeing the doctor! More than anything, I was really concerned about how I'd get Byron back down the stairs without John's help. He got up and pulled on his jacket. At that moment, the receptionist called us in.

John came in with us, met the specialist, and then said he had to leave. As he left the consult room, I made a parting comment about calling emergency services to help get Byron down the stairs.

The visit with the specialist was quick and to the point. By the end of the appointment, we were conversing easily. We talked briefly about the challenge it had been coming up the stairs. As we stood up to leave, the specialist stood up and said, "I'll help you."

Though I protested and said we would attempt the stairs on our own, the doctor took Byron's arm. He headed right through the still-crowded waiting room, past the receptionist's desk, and through the door of the office. I followed as the doctor and Byron walked on.

When we got to the top of the stairs, the doctor asked Byron and me the best way to have Byron hold on to him. I explained that Byron had a very strong grip, and would hold on very firmly in whatever scenario they chose. The doctor didn't seem concerned. He looped Byron's one arm around his neck and placed his own arm around Byron's waist. Then they started down.

I stayed in front of them, hypothetically to catch them if they lost their balance. Byron held tightly to the railing with his one hand, and with the other arm—the arm around the doctor's neck—he held on for dear life. I kept looking back and up at the two of them, making sure everything was okay. All I could see was the death-grip Byron had on this poor man's neck. I could tell Byron was squeezing very firmly because the specialist's face was turning red. I asked if everything was okay, but the doctor kept saying, "We're fine," and continued on.

When we finally reached the landing on the main floor, the doctor disentangled himself from Byron's strong arms.

"Would you like help out to your vehicle, Mrs. Baergen?" he asked me.

I assured him we'd be fine on our own. I was certain the doctor had been brought to the brink of asphyxiation by Byron's neck hold, and I could still picture that room full of patients awaiting him upstairs.

The doctor thanked us for coming in, then turned and headed back up. I had the feeling some elevator maintenance company would momentarily be getting a phone call with some pretty strong words!

As we left that day, I carried with me two very different impressions. One was of the receptionist who couldn't be bothered to deal with anything beyond her official responsibilities. The other was of this doctor, this specialist with a full day and a full waiting room; he'd become so connected with Byron that his sense of compassion superseded the demands of an overflowing waiting room. He was willing to put aside his own schedule to become a walking care aid, helping my son navigate three flights of stairs because the elevator was out.

We've seen Byron have a similar impact on all types of people time and time again. This young man, who is to a great extent dependent upon those around him, continues to regularly touch the lives of people. Whether they have just met him or have known him a long time, Byron's authenticity and singular pursuit of his purpose rubs off on those around him. Many are touched significantly. Byron has what most of us don't have: clarity of purpose. He knows he's got work to do. No matter what spins him around, and oblivious to the reality he is living out, Byron keeps turning back to what he believes is his mission in life.

Byron keeps his end goal in mind almost all the time. I believe that makes an incredible contribution to the way he impacts those around him. We saw this played out again during his recent medical setbacks.

We'd hoped surgery would be averted when God answered our prayers and lowered Byron's dangerously high eye pressure. But that was not to be. The pressure built again and, within a month, Byron was admitted for surgery in both eyes. Because initial consultations had focused on his brain rather than on his eyes, his peripheral vision was greatly damaged by the time of his surgery.

Because of Byron's limitations, recovery room staff asked us to be with him when he returned from the operating room. We stood with the nurses beside his bed as he slowly awoke. We'd seen Byron's impact on the people around him throughout the short hospital experience. We saw it when he showed a calm, friendly spirit during admission; we saw it when the anaesthetist chatted with him, explaining all that was about to happen; and we saw it when we prayed with Byron as he was about to be rolled into the OR.

But it was Byron's own words as he came out of the general anaesthetic which made the most lasting impact. When I heard them, I realized they were a direct echo of what he'd said all those years ago when he found out his friend and life coach Denny had died. In fact, these three simple phrases have been foundational for Byron. By recalling them regularly, he writes them into the unwritten portion of his life.

I believe Byron's words best summarize all we've been trying to say in this book.

So, what did he say? As Byron awakened, he was talking to himself—coaching himself out of the darkness into the light. Nurses were moving in and out of the room, checking to make sure Byron had what he needed to rebound from the surgery, and all of us in the room could hear the voice from the bed. Gradually, Byron's voice became clearer and louder, and each of us could understand the three phrases he uttered again, and again, and again.

"I have courage."

"I am not quitting."

"I am not finished yet."

Amen to that, Byron. You and me both.

When the Greater Dream seems more like the greatest fallacy, let me, too, be able to say, "I have courage"—courage to allow myself to be broken, to trust in God and His work in my life rather than becoming merely bent in my own strength. When life presses me down and everything I see tries to make me believe God has gone silent for good, may I, too, be able to say, "I am not quitting." And when I am tempted to stop making the small but good decisions every day—tempted to throw down the pen and not bother writing good values and foundations into my life—let me remember that even though my tomorrows are still unwritten, what I do today *really* counts. Let me, too, be able to say, "I am not finished yet!"

And what comes next is up to you…

Musings

Epilogue

We look at the blank page before us... life has changed so much since we turned that page. It's amazing what can happen even within one year!

As we stand at yet another crossroad, we are struck by the reality that the rest of our story, the years left to live, will be much shorter than the pages already written. At the same time, our first Encounter God retreat has certainly placed an assurance in us that this is the path God has laid out. We know the full breadth of our ministry experience has prepared us for this, and we also know that the values written on the earlier pages of our story have lain the foundation that now enables us to face new challenges.

We invite you to continue your journey with us for another year! Allow God to meet you, as He has met so many who have felt the love and healing touch of Jesus at an Encounter God Retreat. The setting is a camp situated on the edge of a beautiful lake. We have dormitory housing with bunk beds in each room. It is totally a camp setting, yet the food is amazing and the environment peaceful.

In the quiet of this place, we can hear God's voice. We are reminded of Jesus' life and ministry. He modelled the importance of retreats for us... it was normal for Him to go to a quiet place, away from the crowds, to be with His Father. Luke 4:42 says, *"Jesus often withdrew to the wilderness for prayer"* (NLT). It is in this quiet that we can hear His voice, speaking affirmation and bringing healing to the broken places in our lives. He speaks His love into the depths of who we are! We come from those places more deeply in love with Him and knowing hope for tomorrow.

The meeting begins. Worship moves us to a place of expectancy; something will happen in this place. Then the question is asked: "What would you like Jesus to do in your life this weekend?" We stop to pray, expecting Jesus to respond in the depths of our hearts.

John and I look across the audience. We see an entire family sitting together, we see couples and singles crossing an age demographic of youth to grandparents. We have heard most of their stories, and truly from young to old each one is on a search for something more in their spiritual journey. The background of each person varies as much as their present place in life... denominational leaders, church leaders, church attendees, and those who have given up on the church. Gathered in one room, this diverse group of people has made a defining decision—the status quo is over and authenticity is in. They are committed to meet Jesus. And that is what Encounter God is about—meeting Jesus and allowing His love to flow into and through our lives.

The first presentation begins, and we know Jesus is there. We sense His presence and know the prayers of our team are being answered. People lean forward to catch every word, yet the message isn't new. Session by session, we see barriers drop and expectations rise.

A rough-hewn cross stands at the front of the room, and quickly we recognize that as our focal point. The cross where Jesus paid it all! Throughout the event, we see participants kneeling at the cross or laying prostrate, allowing Jesus love to wash over them. They meet Jesus there.

On Sunday morning, just before we move into the last session, retreat participants are given the opportunity to tell their story, but the guidelines are clear. Comments are to relate only to this retreat and how Jesus has met them and is bringing healing into their journey. A deeper journey has begun for many, but for others, the story of life change may only unfold over time. But we can tell, the deeper work of Jesus has begun.

The final presentation of the retreat concludes and the prayer team ministers into the early hours of the afternoon.

Jesus is the counsellor throughout the weekend. It is profound and amazing to hear Jesus speak. The words from John 10 come to life—"My sheep, hear my voice."

In the midst of the conversation and prayer, Jesus showed us something else. It was about Byron. Because we were unable to get respite for the second retreat, Byron joined us. At about his bedtime, we offered to help him to his room so that he could go to bed. He refused to leave, and then we noticed the impact of his presence there. One pastor, sitting next to Byron, asked Byron to pray for him. Of course, Byron's prayers are not audible, but he bowed his head and did not lift it again until the room had cleared. And that became Byron's role—to pray throughout the weekend. Byron is now a member of our prayer team, and we will never again look for respite. God shows up when Byron is there.

When the event concludes, we stand for the closing prayer. Across the room are people who have experienced the love and healing touch of Jesus. We have all begun a journey together, and we still need each other to continue the journey.

We announce the Encounter Village, the weekly gathering of those who attended the retreat, to begin the next evening. At the Village, we will continue the authentic journey we have begun together. Truth has been spoken into the lives of many who before had come to believe the lies of the enemy. The past no longer need hold them captive; Jesus has brought freedom! Now, together over a potluck dinner, we share our week's journey. We see Jesus continue His work of love and healing. We journey together, enjoying the reality of authentic community, accepting each other regardless of our pasts, and imparting grace even when we experience setbacks. Everyone shares the expectation that there is hope for the greater dream—for all of us!

After one recent Encounter Village prayer time, one team member made an astounding statement. Reaching out cupped hands, he said, "This 'thing' we are holding and nurturing doesn't belong to us. It belongs to the church."

That had been our original dream for Encounter God. We didn't want to just exist alongside the church; we wanted to be fully enveloped in the essence of local churches everywhere. We wanted to fully and completely be *part* of the local church!

Our team member's statement reminded us again that God's call on us is for the church. Recently, we have found ourselves working with leaders of churches. This often leads to invitations to connect with whole staff bodies. Now we are moving from holding retreats at offsite locations, where we've had to invite people to attend, to being booked to hold retreats right in local churches as part of their overall community.

That growing hunger for more of Jesus continues to propel us forward. Since finishing *Unwritten*, our journey forward has not slowed down at all. Our next steps are already clearly laid out:

- Brent and his wife Sabrina are moving their family to Steinbach, Manitoba, for one or two years of intense on-the-job training geared toward preparing them to serve in the national leadership of Encounter God. The church team they will be joining is the place where this journey first began. This church has become a wonderful support and resource base for us, and we are delighted that Brent and Sabrina will be missionaries-in-training there.

- John and I will continue to connect with church leaders across the country, sharing the stories of the significant life changes we've witnessed through Jesus' love and healing touch at Encounter God. As this conversation continues to grow among church leaders across our nation, we want those who serve in local churches to see how effectively Jesus can still work with people who reach for Him.

- Byron will continue to journey alongside us as we move forward with Encounter God. He most often sits in the front row, head bowed as people all around him move into prayer.

He usually refuses to leave the meeting room until everyone else has left.

Byron continues to teach us a great deal about our own relationships with Jesus. As an adult in his thirties now, he still deals with significant issues. A lack of peripheral vision means that things we take for granted can become big challenges for him—standing at the top of the stairs, trying to build up his courage to step forward and down even though he's in the middle of a black void, can become overwhelming for him. Many times, I've seen him hesitate and heard him say, "No, no..." Then I reach out to help him and say, "Byron, when you can't see, you have to trust."

As John and I press forward with Encounter God, as we wrestle with knowing what to do next, I'll hear that same phrase echoed back to me as God whispers in my ear, "Lorraine, when you can't see what's ahead, you have to trust."

Trust. That's the life we've come to embrace. That's the thing about our unwritten pages of tomorrow... we have to continue trusting in a God who can see the way ahead. He is faithful to take our hand and lead us forward.

That's where we're at since finishing *Unwritten*. We're still walking one day at a time, learning what it means to Encounter God afresh every day, and seeing John 14:12—"Anyone who has faith in me will do what I have been doing. He will do even greater things than these" (NIV)—come to life on each fresh and unwritten page.

What's next for you?

Musings

Acknowledgements

Our thanks to those who made this book a reality…

Unwritten has been years in process! The thought was never far from our minds, yet the actual reality of putting pen to paper was more of a distant dream. When God placed someone in our lives who agreed to journey with us, we knew the time had come to seriously delve into the project. We are ever so grateful to God for holding us strong, giving us recall for stories worth passing on, and providing clarity of thought throughout the writing. He allowed the circumstances of life to take us deeper, into another place of spiritual experience, and that in itself has changed the book. We are not the same coming as we were going in. Jesus has changed us, and for that we are grateful.

We are greatly indebted to our writer, Malcolm Petch. He stepped into a role that neither he nor we fully understood. The journey has been much more challenging than we ever imagined. We have stretched him greatly. It was a great learning process for all of us, yet Malcolm has always risen above and stayed faithful to the end. I wonder how many times he might have wanted to throw down his pen, how many times he might have inwardly groaned at yet another rewrite, and still he arrived at the next meeting with a smile. Forever we are grateful to Malcolm as he has lived out his faith before us!

It was through the inspiration of our nephew and his wife, Gordon & Kim Schmidt, that the first printing of *Unwritten* received it's cover. They interrupted their busy professional lives at Gordon Schmidt Photography and Kim Lee Designs to significantly help craft what became the cover of the first edition.

So many more have played a part in this project. First of all, thanks to John & Susan Vawter, who deeply cared about Byron and allowed us to enjoy their Scottsdale home as we gained new strength and refreshment for the journey. Many other friends have also participated in the editing process: Alvina Block, Tuck & Leslie Warner, Roy & Caroline Bouman, Bryan & Gloria Perrier, Gerda Vogt, Sabrina Baergen, Lawrence & Vickie Tomalty, Bruce Heroux, and Arie & Grace Roscher. These friends have sacrificed their time and truly added value to the project. Their insights and suggestions have made the product of this journey one that we believe God will use to impact lives for eternity. We are so thankful for friends whose gifts enlarged what we initially saw.

As we reflect on the past twenty years of life and ministry, a couple who has encouraged us, challenged us to greatness, and partnered with us is Henry & Irene Hamm. Without their belief in us, the greater dream currently unfolding may never have been realized, and this story may have played out quite differently. We are forever grateful to them.

Beyond those who directly assisted us with the project are numerous pastors and leaders who encouraged us to tell our story. Their encouragement gave us the courage to dare to begin.

Family experienced so much life with us. Each has in some way reached out to us, and their touch has enabled us to make this journey. We specifically thank Lorraine's mom, who was always available to hang out with Byron as we worked on the project. We include Rolland Frayne with family, because that is how we feel about him. Rolland regularly directs Byron's workout program, and many days while we were working on the book Byron was in the gym with him.

There are so many more people who have influenced our life and story. How can we begin to highlight each one? Yet we are grateful for each relationship.

You are the recipient of God's love, through the people who touched our lives.

About the Authors

John and Lorraine Baergen live in Kelowna, British Columbia. Their son Byron lives with them on the same piece of country property as his brother, the "sister" who he loves, and his three nephews.

John and Lorraine, together with Brent and Sabrina, give leadership to the Encounter God movement that is extending outside the world of their mentors, Ray and Fran Duerksen. That is where this message began, and it was through their ministry that God brought wholeness and freedom to the Baergen family. The Baergens believe the message of Encounter God is foundational to a new expression of spiritual formation that is emerging, and therefore the time to share this message is *now*.

Meeting Jesus in a personal way makes all the difference in a Christian's life! John and Lorraine hold to the conviction that when leaders lead out of wholeness and freedom, there is no limit to what God can accomplish through their ministry; then, when a community of believers lives out of wholeness and freedom, there is no limit to the difference God can make in their community and beyond. The Baergens provide leadership to a community of believers within the local church setting who have experienced Encounter God, and this "Encounter Village" shares the journey of living through brokenness so God can bring greater wholeness and fullness.

To contact John and Lorraine Baergen, simply email:

lorraine.baergen@shaw.ca

For more information regarding Encounter God, email lorraine@ unwrittenministries.com or call 250-317-4463, or visit unwritten-ministries.com and follow the Encounter God link.

Speaking engagements are available on topics that include:

- Brokenness that Makes One Whole

- Bitterness or Freedom—That Is the Choice

- Hope for Your Marriage

- Self-Leadership

Weekend Retreats on topics that include:

- Brokenness that Makes One Whole

- Bitterness or Freedom—That Is the Choice

- Marriage that Lasts

- Self-Leadership

Elder Retreats or Discussions:

- The Leader's Marriage

- Creating Community in an Alone World